Developing
STUDENT
OWNERSHIP

Developing
STUDENT
OWNERSHIP

Supporting Students to Own
Their Learning through the Use of
Strategic Learning Practices

ROBERT CROWE AND JANE KENNEDY

1400 Centrepark Blvd., Ste. 1000
West Palm Beach, FL 33401
717.845.6300
email: pub@learningsciences.com
learningsciences.com

Printed in the United States of America

22   21   20   19   18   1   2   3   4   5

Publisher's Cataloging-in-Publication Data
provided by Five Rainbows Cataloging Services

Names: Crowe, Robert, author. | Kennedy, Jane, author.
Title: Developing student ownership : supporting students to own their learning through
    the use of strategic learning practices / Robert Crowe [and] Jane Kennedy.
Description: West Palm Beach, FL : Learning Sciences, 2018.
Identifiers: LCCN 2018957881 | ISBN 978-1-943920-55-6 (pbk.) |
    ISBN 978-1-943920-56-3 (ebook)
Subjects: LCSH: Education. | Academic achievement. | Classroom management. |
    Student participation in curriculum planning. | Teacher-student relationships. |
    BISAC: EDUCATION / Classroom Management. | EDUCATION / Professional
    Development. | EDUCATION / Learning Styles.
Classification: LCC LC71.2 .C76 2018 (print) | LCC LC71.2 (ebook) | DDC
    371.207--dc23.

TABLE OF CONTENTS

2 Instruction **47**
Developing Students to Own How They Are Learning

3 Assessment **85**
Developing Students to Own How Well They Are Learning

4 Climate 121
Developing Students to Own Their Role in the Class

Conclusion 155

Motivating Students to Own Their Learning

Bibliography . . . .

ABOUT THE AUTHORS

Robert Crowe

Bob is a cofounder of Elevated Achievement Group, a professional development company dedicated to helping educators develop student ownership at all grade levels. The focus on student ownership is reflective of his experiences in the professional development world. Bob began his tenure in education as a bilingual teacher in California in 1993, when he taught English learners at all proficiency levels. He then began working directly with teachers with a national company. He has worked across the United States supporting administrators, teachers, students, and parents at all school levels to implement standards-based curriculum, instruction, and assessment. It was during these eighteen years as an instructional coach that he saw the value in motivating students to own their learning.

Jane Kennedy

Jane is a cofounder of Elevated Achievement Group. She founded this professional development company with the express desire to focus on supporting educators as she feels they need to be supported—with a collaborative approach instead of a top-down approach. Jane began her career in 1991 on the East Coast as a self-contained classroom teacher in an inner-city, urban setting. This initial experience infused Jane with a passion for educational equity that has influenced her subsequent career focus. This focus led her to begin consulting work with a national textbook publisher, where she supported adults at all levels in the educational system.

ACKNOWLEDGMENTS

We would like to thank our friends and fellow educators for supporting our work in developing authentic student ownership, specifically the outstanding students, teachers, and administrators at the following districts and schools:

- **ACT Academy Cyber Charter High School:** Philadelphia, Pennsylvania

- **Ad Prima Charter Schools:** Philadelphia, Pennsylvania

- **Austin Independent School District:** Austin, Texas

- **California State University, San Bernardino GEAR UP:** San Bernardino, California

- **Chicago Public Schools, Career and Technical Education:** Chicago, Illinois

- **East Palo Alto Academy, Sequoia Union High School District:** East Palo Alto, California

- **Fallbook Union Elementary School District:** Fallbrook, California

- **Fullerton Joint Union High School District:** Fullerton, California

- **Glen A. Wilson High School, Hacienda La Puente Unified School District:** Hacienda Heights, California

- **Harambee Institute of Science & Technology Charter School:** Philadelphia, Pennsylvania

- **Komarek School District 94:** North Riverside, Illinois

- **San Bernardino City Unified School District:** San Bernardino, California

- **Santa Maria High School, Santa Maria Joint Union High School District:** Santa Maria, California
- **Trabuco Hills High School, Saddleback Valley Unified School District:** Mission Viejo, California
- **Walnut Valley Unified School District:** Walnut, California
- **Winslow Township School District:** Atco, New Jersey
- **Youngstown City School District:** Youngstown, Ohio

DEDICATIONS

To Jolene Combs,
my high school journalism teacher at Redondo Union High School,
who supported me to own my role in my writing

To Susan Deans Smith,
my thesis advisor at the University of Texas,
who supported me to own my role in my thinking

To Libby Smith,
my mentor teacher at Yukon Intermediate School,
who supported me to own my role in my teaching

To all of them for supporting me to own my role in my learning

THANK YOU, BOB

To the friends, family, and colleagues
who have supported me on this journey

THANK YOU, JANE

INTRODUCTION

The Look and Sound of Student Ownership

Imagine walking into a third-grade classroom and asking a student, "What are you learning today?"

The student says, "We're reading *Charlotte's Web*."

It's a perfectly acceptable answer but one that does not convey much about the context, content, or skills associated with the learning.

Now imagine asking the question again and hearing this: "Today I am learning how to describe characters by their traits, motivations, and feelings. We are reading *Charlotte's Web*, and I am describing Wilbur in chapter 3. I will know that I have done a good job taking notes on this by filling out my character map accurately. I am learning how to do this because, when we finish the book, I am writing an opinion essay on which character was most admirable: Charlotte, Wilbur, or Fern. I will take notes on all of the characters to use as details in my essay. I am checking with my friends in my group because they will help me figure out if I have left any important information out of my notes. I will help them because that's how we help everybody in the class get smarter. I like working in groups because the talking helps me better understand what I am thinking. I like this classroom because I get smarter every day."

Imagine if that were the response from the majority of the classmates.

Is such an in-depth understanding of one's learning achievable, or is it merely a pipe dream? Do you believe that a child could know that much about what they were learning and how they were learning it? Or know if they were struggling and how to help others with the same learning? Do you believe a student could take this much ownership of their own learning?

We do.

Why Taking Ownership Matters

After over twenty-five years in the classroom, we have seen all types of students take *ownership* of their learning. They are not merely passengers in their education but active participants. Taking ownership allows them to increase their academic achievements across the board—not just in a specific content area.

Years ago, John Hattie (2001) showed us that students who own their learning are more motivated to learn, and those students who are more motivated to learn actually learn more: "It is students themselves, in the end, not teachers, who decide what students will learn. Thus we must attend to what students are thinking, what their goals are, and why they would want to engage in learning what is offered in schools" (p. viii).

But student ownership is almost impossible to develop without teachers. Teachers play a crucial role in ensuring that students recognize their role in learning.

The most effective way for students to understand their role in learning is to get them to take ownership—a skill that can be directly taught and mastered. This book answers the following fundamental questions about teaching students to own their learning:

- ▶ What is student ownership?
- ▶ What does ownership look like and sound like in the classroom?
- ▶ What is the teacher's role in student ownership?
- ▶ What are the most critical supports needed to develop student ownership?

We are sharing the information in this book because we want you to imagine a scenario in which every student in an algebra class is able to report not only that they are learning how to interpret mathematical expressions but also that they are doing so while building on prior knowledge in an environment of collaboration and support, with the result being a learning product that clearly shows their mastery of the skill.

We want you to imagine the same level of ownership from an eighth-grade history class in which students are learning how to cite textual evidence from a primary source or from a high school biology class focused on constructing an evidence-based model and explanation of the structure of DNA.

We want you to imagine the best for your students.

Moving Beyond Doing and Understanding

As teachers, we mentally categorize students into those who do the work and those who do not. Translated into academic language, students are either motivated or not. It follows that students are similarly categorized into those who achieve and those who do not. Commonly heard complaints include the following:

▸ "When I ask them if they understand or have any questions, they just stare at me."

▸ "They wait for me to give them the answer."

▸ "Juliana is the only one who raises her hand, so I always call on her."

▸ "If they don't get it right the first time, they give up."

▸ "Good luck trying to get them to do work at home."

Motivation, to many, is a finite trait. Some kids have it and some don't. But this thinking maintains the status quo. This type of thinking ignores that motivation can be cultivated, so students aren't taught to be motivated. They are left to their own devices rather than shown a better way.

In other words, rather than taking ownership of their learning, many students coast through their education *doing* school. Some begin *understanding* school, but most are unclear about *owning* their learning.

All too often, students are just *doing* school. They come most days, they attend class, they do the work (most of the time), but they don't have a clear reason why they are there—aside from the fact that they are supposed to be there. This is a passive student—they "get" or "don't get" a certain subject, they don't *earn* grades but are given them, and they graduate (or not) based on outside forces. This is a student who knows how to do school but not that their role is to learn.

In addition, some students are better at *understanding* school. They attend classes and finish all of the assignments because they know that this is how to get a good grade. These students are focused on content knowledge and do well when asked to share information and facts. A student who understands school does well in almost all classes because they know what is expected from them. These are students who feel successful in school but have little clarity about learning. They'd struggle explaining the skills they are learning, why they are learning these skills, or how they will use these skills in the future. In other words, they are missing the thinking piece that is going to advance their learning.

True success in education requires that students to go beyond just *doing* or *understanding* school—they must *own* their learning. A student who owns their learning can state what they are learning and why, can explain how they learn best, can articulate when they are learning and when they are struggling, and understands their role in any academic setting. Asking a student who is fully invested in the ownership of their learning will give an answer like that third-grade student reading *Charlotte's Web*.

Thus, student ownership is best defined as a mindset. Students with an ownership mindset know they have the authority, the capacity, and the responsibility to own their learning.

Building Authority, Capacity, and Responsibility

How can we as teachers support our students to cultivate an ownership mindset? By delegating the authority, the capacity, and the responsibility to them.

Successful students will have the **authority** to make decisions regarding their own learning. This doesn't mean that they are free to decide what they want to learn solely based on their interests. This would not prepare them to explore content they have never been exposed to. Instead, this means that, when they are learning something new, they have the authority to determine what they need in order to master that skill—for example, frequency and types of practice, specific opportunities to authentically apply learning, and more opportunities to transfer learning into new situations. It is the role of teachers to ensure that students have the authority to make decisions about how they learn.

Students must also have the **capacity** to own their learning. They have capacity when teachers provide them with the knowledge and skills to challenge themselves and self-reflect on their growth. These are the skills that lead to metacognition. Capacity is built by supplying students with the skills needed to succeed, share why they need them, and explain how they will use them in their current and future learning. Once students have the authority to make decisions about how they will learn, it is the role of teachers to ensure that they have the capacity to analyze and reflect on their own learning.

Finally, students must have the **responsibility** to be held accountable for their own academic achievements. Students must understand their role in their own learning and take responsibility for their successes as well as their mistakes. But they can't be held responsible if they have no understanding of what they are learning, how they will be taught, and how they will demonstrate their learning. Educators cannot demand that students take responsibility of their learning if they have not given them the authority and the capacity to do so.

So, how does a teacher build the authority, capacity, and responsibility needed for student ownership? A teacher must model the thinking behind the ownership, explicitly teach the skills of ownership, and, most importantly, be willing to delegate the authority, capacity, and responsibility to the students.

So much has been written about the need for students to be more motivated and how, if this singular goal can be achieved, motivation will lead to greater academic success. We couldn't agree more. However, not much has been written about how students can be explicitly and directly *taught* to be more motivated. That is where this book comes in. It will directly show teachers how to increase motivation, and thus achievement, by increasing student ownership.

The Strategic Learning Practices of Student Ownership

Using a variety of research about what best supports students to increase ownership of their learning, we have developed a set of strategic learning practices to be offered to students on a daily basis.

These practices are the actions that offer students the most opportunities to increase their learning—they offer support for students as they are given the authority, capacity, and responsibility to own their learning. The practices are strategic because the teacher must strategically and methodically determine when and how to offer these supports. Because the teacher is the person in the school who knows the most about the students, it is important that the teacher be allowed to determine when to offer supports to the students. These practices focus on increasing learning. While there are hundreds of actions a teacher must take in a day, this book focuses on those practices in curriculum, instruction, assessment, and climate that actually increase the opportunities for learning—and increase the opportunities for student ownership.

Chapter 1 will focus on the best practices regarding curriculum. Curriculum is defined as what the student needs to know and be able to do at the end of a lesson, unit, or course. To demonstrate increased student ownership in curriculum, the goal is for each and every student to clearly articulate answers to the following questions:

- ▶ What am I learning?
- ▶ Why am I learning this?
- ▶ How will I demonstrate I have learned it?

This means that the teacher must begin by determining the answers to the following questions:

- ▶ What will my students learn?
- ▶ Why are my students learning this?
- ▶ How will my students demonstrate they have learned it?

Curriculum begins with understanding the content and skills a student needs to master in order to be successful. In terms of the state standards, curriculum is the content and skills students must master to be ready for college and a career. Thus, curriculum includes the standards and the learning objectives constructed from the state's expectations. However, curriculum is more than the standards. It also includes the materials and resources students will interact with to master that content and those skills.

Curriculum must also include the demonstration of learning that shows a student has mastered that standard or skill. This demonstration must be measurable and observable so that both the teacher and student can monitor progress.

In order to answer the preceding questions, teachers must decide which standard (or standards) to focus on, which learning outcomes students will master and in what order, what mastery looks like and sounds like, what materials and resources students need to use and interact with, and how this learning connects to previous and subsequent learning.

Chapter 2 will focus on the best practices in instruction. Instruction is defined as the strategies students will use to learn the skills determined in curriculum. To demonstrate increased student ownership in instruction, the goal is for each and every student to articulate the following:

- ▸ How will I learn this?
- ▸ How will this strategy help me learn this?
- ▸ How can I use this strategy in the future and in different situations?

Understanding the process for learning leads to increased metacognition and allows students to own their most effective and efficient learning style. Thus, the teacher must decide the following:

- ▸ How will my students learn this?
- ▸ How will this strategy help my students learn this?
- ▸ How will my students use this strategy in the future and in different situations?

Instruction begins with understanding that different methodologies can be employed to deliver information to students. Because there is such a variety in the content and skills students need to learn, delivery can fall anywhere on the continuum from structured to open-ended. While the decision regarding the delivery method is the teacher's to make, it cannot be made without a clear understanding of the learner.

In order to answer the preceding questions, teachers must decide which delivery method best addresses the content or skill of the standard or learning outcome, the needs of the students, the various learning styles in the classroom, and the sequence in which the learning falls (in the lesson, unit, or course).

Chapter 3 will focus on the best practices regarding in-class assessment. Assessment is defined as the student's ability to know when they are learning and when they are struggling. To demonstrate increased student ownership in assessment, the goal is for each and every student to clearly answer the following questions:

▸ How will I know I have learned it?

▸ How will I know I am progressing in my learning?

▸ What can I do if I am struggling?

Thus, the teacher must decide how to answer the following:

▸ How will my students know they have learned this?

▸ How will my students know they are progressing in their learning?

▸ What can my students do if they are struggling?

Assessment begins with understanding that mastery of a specific content or skill must be concrete to both the teacher and the student. A teacher will have a difficult (if not impossible) task if they are trying to teach something that does not have a clear and defined end. A student will struggle (if not give up) when the end is unclear or when they are unaware of what they have to do to show that they have learned. However, assessment is more than just the end or final product. It also includes knowing what each step along the way looks like and how supportive each step is to the mastery of the broader content or skill.

In order to answer the preceding question—"How will my students know they have learned this?"—teachers must decide what mastery of that content or skill looks like, the different ways students can independently demonstrate this mastery, which way best expresses mastery of the standard or learning outcome at a discrete level, and which way best expresses mastery of the standard or learning outcome at the application and transference level.

In order to answer the other questions—"How will my students know they are progressing in their learning?" and "What can my students do if they are struggling?"—teachers must decide how to periodically check for understanding; offer constructive, affirming, or corrective feedback; and adjust the instruction when it isn't working for the students. This supports students by acknowledging that new learning is not achieved in a straight line but that new learning can be circuitous, even daunting, at times.

Chapter 4 will focus on the best practices to build a positive academic climate. **Climate** is defined as a student-centered environment that accelerates student learning. To demonstrate increased student ownership in climate, the goal is for each and every student to answer the following:

- ▸ What is my role in the class?

- ▸ How will I support others in their learning?

- ▸ How will I take risks in my learning?

This means the teacher must form answers to the following questions:

- ▸ What is the student's role in the class?

- ▸ How will my students support others in their learning?

- ▸ How will my students take risks in their learning?

Building a positive classroom climate is crucial if students are to take risks in their learning. And taking risks is a demonstration that students are increasing the ownership of their own learning. This positive climate determines how students receive feedback from the teacher and one another, how students work together to enhance one another's learning, and how students support one another to take risks with their learning.

In order to answer the preceding questions, teachers must decide how to directly teach cooperation and collaboration, how to offer authentic opportunities for students to work together, how to model that making mistakes is an integral part of learning something new, and how to deliver feedback that is respectful, supportive, and that promotes the student's self-worth while moving the student toward accuracy and understanding.

Why Increasing Ownership Elevates Achievement

Not one of these decisions regarding curriculum, instruction, assessment, and climate can be made in isolation. Each decision will impact other decisions. It is the teacher's job to decide how these four areas work together to ensure that there is the highest likelihood of student learning. Thus, the teacher's greatest power is in their decision-making. Decisions such as the sequence of a course, the focus of a unit, the goal of a lesson, the selection of an instructional strategy, and the assessment of student mastery lie in the teacher's hands. That these decisions support increased student ownership is paramount.

With increased student ownership comes elevated student achievement. Focusing on and being strategic with the practices that will support student ownership will allow students to achieve more and to a higher degree.

Let's revisit that third-grade classroom. This is a clear example of a class where students own their learning. These students can articulate what they are learning, why they are learning it, how they will demonstrate they have learned it, how they are learning it, and how they will work as a class to support one another.

As the student said: "I like this classroom because I get smarter every day."

For each and every student, that's the best motivation.

1 CURRICULUM

Developing Students to Own What They Are Learning

For many teachers, planning starts with the curriculum—that is, what is taught, the resources that are used, the materials that need to be covered. This tends to be focused on what the teacher needs to do as guided by the pacing map or the textbook. In many cases the curriculum is content-driven: in language arts it's the literature (*Romeo and Juliet*), in history or science it's the topic (ancient Greece or volcanoes and earthquakes), and in math it's solving problems (two-digit addition).

This approach to curriculum tends to make the teacher focus on what they have to *teach* today. We need to flip this focus on what students need to *learn* today, tomorrow, and for the rest of the year. True student ownership begins when the teacher looks at curriculum from the student's point of view.

Curriculum is defined as what the student needs to know and be able to do at the end of a lesson, unit, and course. Students are more supported to own their learning when all learning is driven by a standards-based curriculum with measurable and achievable outcomes. This is different from content-driven curriculum in which the teacher tries to "finish the book" before the end of the year. Instead, a standards-based curriculum is student-focused, incorporating outcomes that define what a student should know (content) and be able to do (skill) by the end of a course, unit, and lesson. For a student to be college and career ready, the greater emphasis must be on what the student should be able to do. Curriculum also includes the materials and resources students will interact with while working to master the content and skills.

The Imperatives for Ownership of Curriculum

To develop student ownership, several things are imperative: It is imperative for students to know and be able to articulate the skills they are mastering in the day's lesson, in the unit, and in the course. It is imperative for students to know and be able to articulate how they will show that they have mastered these skills. It is imperative that they know and are able to articulate why they are learning these skills, how they will apply them in the course, and how they will transfer the skills into other situations. It is imperative that they are able to listen, speak, read, and write about these skills. It is imperative that they know and are able to articulate where they are in the learning process—initial learning, practicing, applying, or transferring. It is imperative that they know and are able to articulate how the materials they are using will help them master the skills at a more rigorous level.

Table 1.1 provides some helpful indicators that reveal when students are taking ownership of their learning.

How Do Students Demonstrate Ownership of Curriculum?

Each and every student is able to articulate:

- what they are learning,
- why they are learning this,
- how they will demonstrate mastery of this learning,
- how applying the learning in a variety of ways–listening, speaking, reading, and writing–supports mastery,
- how the current learning relates to previous and subsequent learning,
- how they can use the learning in the future,
- what curriculum materials they are using,
- how these materials support the learning,
- what other materials they could use in the future to continue this learning, and
- why articulating these aspects of curriculum helps them own their learning.

Table 1.1: Indicators of Student Ownership of Curriculum

For students to be able answer questions about what they are learning, they need to know the plan for their learning. Thus, it is crucial for teachers to know where they are heading. Grant Wiggins and Jay McTighe (2005) recognize the value of backward mapping: "Plan with the end in mind by first clarifying the learning you seek—the learning results. Then, think about the assessment evidence needed to show that students have achieved that desired learning. Finally, plan the means to the end—the teaching and learning activities and resources to help them achieve the goals. We have found that backward design, whether applied by individual teachers or district curriculum committees, helps avoid the twin sins of activity-oriented and coverage-oriented curriculum planning" (p. 7).

Teachers who backward plan have the ability to tell their students what they are learning, when they are learning it, how they will apply the learning, and how they will continue revisiting the learning to deepen their understanding, thus giving students the opportunity to own their learning.

Putting Student Ownership into Practice

But what does student ownership look like in practice? What does it sound like when a student owns their part in curriculum? What is the difference between a student who is simply *doing* or *understanding* curriculum and one who is *owning* what they are learning?

A student is *doing* when they can state the task in front of them or recite what they are doing.

A student is *understanding* when they can explain the skill they are learning.

A student is *owning* when they can articulate what skill they are learning, why they are learning it, how they will demonstrate they have learned it, and how they will use it in the future.

The tables that follow—table 1.2, table 1.3, table 1.4, and table 1.5—present some examples of what this looks and sounds like on a continuum of doing-understanding-owning in a variety of content areas and grade levels, particularly when we ask the question, "What are you learning?"

Possible responses on the continuum from first grade
students in English-language arts when asked,

"What are you learning?"

"We are
learning to use details
from the story to describe
the characters. They help us
understand the character better.
When I write a story, I make sure to
include details about my characters.
And now, when I read other stories,
I use details to help me understand
them better. I get to practice this a lot
because the teacher reads to us
and we have a lot of books to
choose from."

"I am drawing pictures
to retell the main
parts of the story."

"We are
reading this
book."

DOING   UNDERSTANDING   OWNING

Table 1.2: Student Ownership Continuum, English-Language Arts, Grade 1

Possible responses on the continuum from
third grade students in science when asked,

"What are you learning?"

"We are
learning about the
cause and effects of evolution.
When changes happen in the
environment, some organisms
survive, some move, and some die.
We are gathering examples of each. I
will be writing an essay about a specific
organism to show whether it would
live, move, or die in different
habitats. I have to use evidence
to support my ideas."

"We are learning
about evolution. When
changes happen, some
organisms survive, some
move, and some die. I
have to read to find
examples of each."

"I am reading
this chapter and
answering."

DOING   UNDERSTANDING   OWNING

Table 1.3: Student Ownership Continuum, Science, Grade 3

*Possible responses on the continuum from
seventh grade students in history when asked,*

"What are you learning?"

"We are
learning about the
relationships between
geographic, political, economic,
religious, and social structures in
various civilizations. In two weeks, we
will put together a slide presentation on
one of the civilizations. Right now, we are
learning how to cite textual evidence.
My document is a map of the Arabian
Peninsula. I will use Cornell notes
to take notes. This will help me
make sure I have accurate
evidence."

"We are learning
about how geography
and climate affected
how people lived. We
are taking notes on
examples of this from
the Middle Ages."

"I am reading
this article."

DOING   UNDERSTANDING   OWNING

Table 1.4: Student Ownership Continuum, History, Grade 7

*Possible responses on the continuum from
high school students in algebra I when asked,*

"What are you learning?"

"We have been learning
how to make approximations
when we are solving problems.
Right now, we are solving some
problems that practice using units
to solve problems. We will use our
approximations and math solutions
with units to justify our answers. I
use the mathematical practice of
approximations to make sure my
thinking is robust and that the
math makes sense."

"We are learning
to use units to
solve problems. We are
practicing solving them
and then comparing our
answers with our partner
to see which ones we
got correct."

"I have to
solve these
problems."

DOING   UNDERSTANDING   OWNING

Table 1.5: Student Ownership Continuum, Algebra I, High School

Moving to Student Ownership

What can a teacher do to move a student toward owning their learning? Student ownership is best defined as a mindset. Students who know they have the authority, capacity, and responsibility to own their learning possess an ownership mindset. Thus, to move a student, the teacher must delegate the authority, build the capacity, and give the responsibility to each and every student.

How does a teacher do this? They must model the thinking behind the ownership and explicitly teach the skills of ownership. This takes planning. In order for students to answer the questions posed earlier—"What am I learning?", "Why am I learning this?", and "How will I demonstrate I have learned it?"—teachers must be strategic in the practices they use to increase learning.

While there are hundreds of actions a teacher must take in a day, we will focus on those three practices in curriculum that research shows increase the opportunities for learning—by increasing the opportunities for student ownership.

Teachers must strategically decide when to offer the following three learning practices:

- **Strategic Learning Practice, Curriculum 1:** Each and every student is supported by relevant standards with measurable and achievable outcomes that are accessible and that drive all learning.

- **Strategic Learning Practice, Curriculum 2:** Each and every student is supported by units and lessons that provide an integrated approach and that support conceptual redundancy of the learning outcomes.

- **Strategic Learning Practice, Curriculum 3:** Each and every student is supported by access to curriculum materials that match the content and rigor of the learning outcomes.

In the following sections, we will clearly define each learning practice, describe what implementation looks and sounds like in the classroom, share teacher planning questions, offer examples of how students have been supported with these learning practices in a variety of content areas and grade levels, and explain how these practices directly lead to increased student ownership.

Strategic Learning Practice, Curriculum 1

Each and Every Student Is Supported by Relevant Standards with Measurable and Achievable Outcomes That Are Accessible and That Drive All Learning

In order for students to own their learning in regard to curriculum, each and every student must be able to answer the following questions:

> ‣ What skill am I learning?
>
> ‣ Why am I learning this skill?
>
> ‣ How will I know I have learned this skill?

In order for teachers to develop students who own their learning in regard to curriculum, it is imperative that teachers support students with practices that are strategically implemented on a daily basis. This requires a focus on those practices that Locke and Latham (1990), Marzano (1998), and Fendick (1990) show increase the opportunities for learning by increasing the opportunities for student ownership. Strategic Learning Practice, Curriculum 1, states: "Each and every student is supported by **relevant standards** with **measurable and achievable outcomes** that are **accessible** and that **drive all learning**."

First, let's define each aspect of this practice.

Relevant standards are the skills or content from the standards that are both appropriate for the student's grade level and for the time of year. The verb or action of the standard is key. Identifying the verb or action helps the teacher recognize the appropriate level of learning, both in terms of where students fall in the course of their education (grade level) and where they fall in the instructional sequence (time of year).

Measurable and achievable outcomes clearly define what students are learning and how they will know they have learned it. *What* students are learning is the skill or content directly derived from the standard. It incorporates the language of the standard itself. *How* students will know they have learned it is directly related to the product or demonstration that shows the learning. This demonstration measures the level of application and is the measurable aspect of the objective. The measurable outcome must be achievable in the time parameters of the lesson.

Outcomes that are **accessible** allow all students to understand and articulate what they are learning, why they are learning it, and how they will know they have learned it. Accessibility is dependent on the student. For example, visual learners will need to read the outcome, auditory learners will need to hear the outcome, and social learners will need to discuss the outcome with peers.

Outcomes that **drive all learning** imply that learning time is precious and should not be squandered. In other words, every minute in the lesson is utilized for the teaching and learning of that outcome.

The Practice in Action

What does this practice—"Each and every student is supported by **relevant standards** with **measurable and achievable outcomes** that are **accessible** and that **drive all learning**"—look like in a classroom at the highest level? You might walk into Mrs. Lavetti's high school American history class and read the following outcome on the board: "Students will connect insights gained from specific details to develop an understanding of a primary source in order to accurately take Cornell notes on Abraham Lincoln's second inaugural address."

But that is what the teacher wrote. What happens when you talk with her students and ask them questions?

You: "What are you learning?"

Student: "I am learning to make connections from specific parts of a text to gain insights about and better understand the primary document, Abraham Lincoln's second inaugural address."

You: "How do you gain insights?"

Student: "I gain insights when I not only look at the parts of a text but also pull the pieces together to understand the document as a whole. In this case, we are looking at the specific details that Abraham Lincoln used and how they connect together to express his larger idea."

You: "How will you know that you have learned this?"

Student: "I will use Cornell notes to accurately cite evidence from Abraham Lincoln's second inaugural address, which I will use later to analyze Lincoln's overall meaning."

You: "What are Cornell notes?"

Student: "Cornell notes are a way to take notes that helps me remember what was in Abraham Lincoln's second inaugural address. There is a place for the main ideas—see, here I have the headings for each of the four paragraphs—and a place for my notes from the speech to remind me what the important ideas are in that section."

You: "Why are you learning this?"

Student: "After we finish reading Abraham Lincoln's second inaugural address, we are going to write an essay about the overall purpose of this speech. Finding specific evidence from this source will help me write a better essay."

Are you wondering how the student was able to answer your questions so clearly and with such confidence? Let's ask Mrs. Lavetti.

"My students did not answer questions at this level because I simply posted a strong objective on the board. I had to intentionally plan how I would support them. First, I needed to know what skill they would learn, how they would show it, how they would use it in the future, and how I would deliver the lesson. I also had to determine how I would explain every step of the way what we are doing—what, how, and why I am teaching and what, how, and why they are learning."

Mrs. Lavetti used the Strategic Learning Practice, Curriculum 1, as a frame to help her plan how she wanted to offer this support. This frame is flexible and fits the needs of both teachers and students. However, the following planning questions in table 1.6 helped her focus the support.

Questions to Guide Implementing Strategic Learning Practice, Curriculum 1:

Each and every student is supported by relevant standards with measurable and achievable outcomes that are accessible and that drive all learning.

Use these planning questions to focus your support.

Notes:

❏ What does the standard call for?

❏ Which component of the standard will students learn in this lesson?

❏ What academically appropriate language will be included?

❏ How will my students demonstrate the learning?

❏ Why are my students learning this skill?

❏ How will I share this information with my students?

❏ How will I check that my students understand the goals of the learning?

❏ How will my students understand that knowing these aspects of the learning will support ownership of their learning?

Table 1.6: Questions to Guide Implementing Strategic Learning Practice, Curriculum 1

Implementing the Practice

How did Mrs. Lavetti use the questions in table 1.6 to help plan how she would offer support to her students? First, she had to ask herself:

- What does the standard call for?
- Which component of the standard will students learn in this lesson?
- What academically appropriate language will be included?

Mrs. Lavetti recalls, "I began by reviewing Reading Standard 1 for Literacy in History/Social Studies at grades 11–12: 'Cite specific textual evidence to support analysis of primary and secondary sources, connecting insights gained from specific details to an understanding of the text as a whole.'

"Then I broke the standard into three teachable parts (the *what*, or the skill aspect of the outcome): (1) cite specific textual evidence to support analysis of primary and secondary sources, (2) connect insights gained from specific details, (3) connect insights gained from specific details to an understanding of the text as a whole.

"I then reviewed the learning progressions for Reading Standard 1 for Literacy in History/Social Studies at the earlier grades to find out what has already been learned."

Mrs. Lavetti then hands you a printout of table 1.7, which follows, so that you can view the progressions quickly and easily.

11-12.RH.1	Cite specific textual evidence to support analysis of primary and secondary sources, connecting insights gained from specific details to an understanding of the text as a whole.
9-10.RH.1	Cite specific textual evidence to support analysis of primary and secondary sources, attending to such features as the date and origin of the information.
6-8.RH.1	Cite specific textual evidence to support analysis of primary and secondary sources.

Table 1.7: Learning Progressions for Reading Standard 1 for Literacy in History/Social Studies

Mrs. Lavetti gestures to the printout and says, "From this, I knew that my students should be able to cite specific evidence to support analysis of primary and secondary sources. The learning in eleventh grade is to continue to practice citing evidence *while* learning to connect insights gained from specific details to an understanding of the text as whole. That is the new learning for my students. This also provides me with what academic language I need to teach."

With those guiding questions to implementing Strategic Learning Practice, Curriculum 1, completed, Mrs. Lavetti next had to determine the following:

▸ How will my students demonstrate the learning?

▸ Why are my students learning this skill?

To answer these questions, she says, "I had to decide what the demonstration of the learning would be. Once my students have analyzed Abraham Lincoln's second inaugural address, they will write an explanatory essay that answers the question: 'What was the overall purpose of Abraham Lincoln's second inaugural address?' As they are reading, they are also gathering evidence for the essay they will write at the end.

"For this lesson, they are reading his address. In the previous lesson, they finished analyzing the state of the country at the time of the inaugural address. Students will need to take explicit notes. My colleagues and I in the department have decided to incorporate Cornell notes in all classes, so those are what students will use to demonstrate mastery of this skill."

Mrs. Lavetti used the planning questions to help her plan the curriculum aspect of her lesson. She is now ready to determine *how* she will teach this, because she knows she has decided the two most crucial aspects of her lesson: (1) the skill her students are learning and (2) the demonstration of the learning.

But that planning is about the lesson. Mrs. Lavetti wants to ensure that her students will own this information so that she can increase the probability of their learning. She must ask herself the following questions:

▸ How will I share this information with my students?

▸ How will I check that my students understand the goals of the learning?

Mrs. Lavetti says, "I have a range of learners in my classroom. I know that, in order for them to own this information, I need to support them in a variety of ways. I introduce the objective at the onset of each lesson, and I review it throughout the lesson as needed. For visual learners the objective is posted, for auditory learners the objective is stated out loud, and for social learners the objective is discussed with peers. Periodically throughout the lesson, I will have students share with a partner and remind each other what they are learning (the skill), how they will know they have learned it (the demonstration), and why they are learning it (future use of the learning)."

Mrs. Lavetti wants to ensure that her eleventh graders understand the value of owning their own learning. Therefore, she has to determine the following:

▶ How will my students understand that knowing these aspects of the learning will support ownership of their learning?

Mrs. Lavetti says her answer to this question involves student participation. "Every day we reflect on our learning. About once a week, I have the students review the learning progressions and rank themselves. The ranking has them determine what skills they could teach to another student, what skills they feel that with a little more practice they would master, and what skills they need more support with. Students themselves are the best at figuring out their own needs."

Teachers like Mrs. Lavetti realize that without this support—focusing on a relevant standard, determining what skill the students will be learning and how they will show they have learned it, having the students know and understand what they are learning, and ensuring the instructional time is used efficiently—her students will struggle with owning their learning.

What Teachers Are Doing

What are other ways teachers have implemented this practice—"Each and every student is supported by **relevant standards** with **measurable and achievable outcomes** that are **accessible** and that **drive all learning**"—as they offer support for developing student ownership?

Take this example from a middle school math teacher: "I sometimes forget to tell my students what they are learning. So, I asked a student—I picked the one who usually doesn't like to pay attention—to monitor the beginning of class. If I haven't told the class the objective of the lesson within five minutes, this student is to raise his hand and ask me to state the objective of the day. This helped him stay on task, it helped me remember to tell my class the

great idea

goal of the lesson, and it modeled for students the value of knowing what they were learning."

Take this example from a high school biology teacher: "I felt like in the past I did a fair job of letting students know what we were learning. However, my work with the strategic learning practices has helped me more effectively communicate my learning goals with students. I start off every class period sharing a Google Slides presentation that gives a clear outcome and communicates what students will be learning, how and why they will be learning it, and how they will demonstrate their learning to me. I've seen how much this has changed my students' success. I regularly poll my students, and in a survey they shared that they really appreciate that I start the period in this way and that I refer back to the outcome throughout the lesson."

Take this example from a seventh-grade Spanish teacher: "We have Chromebooks at my school, and I post my lessons every day. I put the learning objective in the footer so it is always accessible during the lesson."

Take this example from a third-grade teacher: "I wouldn't be able to plan for the relevant standard and turn it into my learning outcome without looking at the reading learning progressions. By looking at these I know that my students should come into my class able to ask and answer questions about a text, demonstrate understanding of key details, and use the question words of *who, what, where, when, why,* and *how.* The new skill in third grade is to refer explicitly to the text as the basis for their answers. Now, if my students aren't proficient in the other skills, I will review those. But understanding what is new for my kids is crucial because this is the new learning for this grade."

Take this example from a high school English teacher: "I'm almost embarrassed to say that, until I read the learning progression in literacy, my students were learning skills at a much lower level. I didn't know better because I never looked at the verbs in the standards. I just looked at content. So when I taught theme, I just taught the concept. It didn't occur to me to understand the difference between identify the theme, determine the theme, and analyze how character, plot, and setting drove the development of the theme. By only looking at the concept, I didn't have my students working at the level of high school rigor."

What Students Are Saying

What do students say about this practice—"Each and every student is supported by **relevant standards** with **measurable and achievable outcomes** that are **accessible** and that **drive all learning**"—and its support for the ownership of their learning?

Take this example from a fourth grader: "I can't own my learning if I don't know what I am learning! So we start the day with what I'm supposed to learn. That really helps me stay on task. Once I can do it on my own, I know that I have learned it. This makes me feel smart."

Take this example from a high school sophomore: "There are so many skills at this level that I can use in all my classes. If the teacher tells me what I am learning in class, I can think if I have ever learned this before, maybe even in a different class, and then I can think about how I would transfer that skill into this class. This helps me save time, and it helps me realize that all skills can be used in more than one class."

Strategic Learning Practice, Curriculum 2

Each and Every Student Is Supported by Units and Lessons
That Provide an Integrated Approach and That Support
Conceptual Redundancy of the Learning Outcomes

In order for students to own their learning in regard to curriculum, each and every student must be able to answer the following questions:

▸ How does learning in a variety of ways—listening, speaking, reading, and writing—support mastery of the skill?

▸ How does the current learning relate to previous and subsequent learning?

▸ How can I use this learning in the future?

In order for teachers to develop students who own their learning in regard to curriculum, it is imperative that teachers support students with practices that are strategically implemented on a daily basis. This requires a focus on those practices that Walker, Greenwood, Hart, and Carta (1994) and Nuthall (2005) show increase the opportunities for learning by increasing the opportunities for student ownership. Strategic Learning Practice, Curriculum 2, states: "Each and every student is supported by **units and lessons** that provide an **integrated approach** and that support **conceptual redundancy** of the learning outcomes."

First, let's define each aspect of this practice.

A **unit** is a series of lessons that are linked together and work toward an authentic, cumulative outcome.

A **lesson** is designed to teach a specific learning outcome as part of a larger unit. A lesson usually has a clear beginning and ending, and it can be driven by a period of time. However, the lesson needs to be framed by students first understanding what they are going to learn (beginning) and then independently demonstrating the learning (ending).

Using an **integrated approach** ensures that students are provided multiple and varied opportunities to grapple with the same skill or concept. This usually includes opportunities to listen about, talk about, read about, and write about the skill or concept. It can also include the use of the practice standards to support mastery of the content standards.

Conceptual redundancy ensures that students have opportunities for repetition with the same concept in a variety of approaches. This includes opportunities to learn the skill initially, practice the skill, apply the skill, and then transfer the skill across time.

The Practice in Action

What does this practice—"Each and every student is supported by **units and lessons** that provide an **integrated approach** and that support **conceptual redundancy** of the learning outcomes"—look like in a classroom at the highest level? You might walk into Mr. Scott's first-grade mathematics class and read the following outcome on the board: "Students will demonstrate their understanding of addition and the meaning of the equal sign in order to accurately identify if addition equations are true or false."

But that is what the teacher wrote. What happens when you talk with his students and ask them questions?

You: "What are you learning?"

Student: "I am learning to show how to use an equal sign. When you add numbers, you have to use an equal sign to show what the numbers add up to. Like two plus two equals four. It has to be true. You can't say two plus two equals five because that is not true. The equal sign is important."

You: "Right now you are demonstrating this learning by talking. What other ways can you can demonstrate this learning?"

Student: "I can also write it. See how I wrote this math sentence, 2 + 4 = 6? We also use our unit blocks to show it. See, I can put two blocks together with four blocks, and when you count them, you now have six blocks. So you can see that two plus four equals six is true. Being able to talk about it, write about it, and model it helps me remember better."

You: "What is a model?"

Student: "A model is when you show your math using things like unit blocks. You can also draw a picture for a model. It helps us see the math."

You: "How does this learning connect to what you learned before today?"

Student: "We already learned to add before and to use our blocks to model our addition sentences."

You: "How will you use this learning after today?"

Student: "We will always use equal signs. We are also learning about sub-traction because it is like addition but different. We also have to use equal signs there. Mr. Scott says we will be adding bigger numbers, and even then we will have to use the equal sign and make sure our math sentences are true."

Are you wondering how the student was able to answer your questions so clearly and with such confidence? Let's ask Mr. Scott.

"My students did not answer questions at this level because I simply posted a strong outcome on the board. I had to intentionally plan how I would support them. First, I needed to know what skill they would learn, how they could apply the learning in a variety of ways, how the learning would connect to previous and subsequent learning, and how the students would be able to use the learning in the future."

He used the Strategic Learning Practice, Curriculum 2, as a frame to help him plan how he wanted to offer this support. This frame is flexible and fits the needs of both teachers and students. However, the following planning questions in table 1.8 helped him focus the support.

Questions to Guide Implementing Strategic Learning Practice, Curriculum 2:

Each and every student is supported by units and lessons that provide an integrated approach and that support conceptual redundancy of the learning outcomes.

Use these planning questions to focus your support.

Notes:

- ❑ What skill will my students learn, and how will they show they have learned it?

- ❑ How does the unit or lesson integrate reading, writing, speaking, and listening?

- ❑ How does the unit or lesson integrate content standards with practice standards?

- ❑ How do I provide conceptual redundancy through multiple interactions with the same concept?

- ❑ How does the lesson tie to the previous learning?

- ❑ How does the lesson build to subsequent learning and future use?

- ❑ How will I share this information with my students?

- ❑ How will I check that my students understand the goals of the learning?

- ❑ How will my students understand that knowing these aspects of the learning support ownership of their learning?

Table 1.8: Questions to Guide Implementing Strategic Learning Practice, Curriculum 2

Implementing the Practice

How did Mr. Scott use the questions in table 1.8 to help plan how he would offer support to his students? First, he had to determine the following:

▸ What skill will my students learn, and how will they show they have learned it?

Mr. Scott says, "I began by reviewing the Math Standard: 'Understand the meaning of the equal sign, and determine if equations involving addition and subtraction are true or false.' I knew that my focus for this lesson was going to be on understanding the equal sign with equations involving addition.

"I then reviewed the standards at the earlier grade to find out what has already been learned. Those standards showed me that my students should be able to solve addition and subtraction problems up to ten and model them in a variety of ways. The learning in grade one is to continue to practice that *while* learning to understand the meaning of the equal sign to determine if equations involving addition and subtraction are true or false. We will also continue to work with larger numbers up to twenty. That is the new learning for my students."

Mr. Scott then had to determine answers to the following questions:

▸ How does the unit or lesson integrate reading, writing, speaking, and listening?

▸ How does the unit or lesson integrate content standards with practice standards?

Mr. Scott continues. "I now had to decide how I would provide my students with ways to hear about, talk about, read about, and write about the new skill. I also needed to make sure to integrate the math content with the practice standards. For this skill, I decided it was a great time to incorporate both the practice of Attend to Precision and Model with Mathematics. It will be important for my students to understand that the equal sign is about precision to ensure their math sentences are accurate. They will use modeling to demonstrate and show the accuracy of the math. I have not planned my instruction yet, but I know my students will have ample opportunities to explain their math learning, to listen to their peers explain their learning, and to model their understanding of the equal sign and addition."

Next, Mr. Scott needed to ask himself the following:

▸ How do I provide conceptual redundancy through multiple interactions with the same concept?

▸ How does the lesson tie to previous learning?

▸ How does the lesson build to subsequent learning and future use?

Mr. Scott says, "I now had to decide how the students would be provided with multiple interactions with the concept. It is equally important that they understand how today's learning connects to what they have already learned and how they will use it in the future. I haven't decided yet how I will teach the lesson, but I know that my students will need several opportunities to practice creating accurate addition sentences using the equal sign. I will have planned structured peer conversations to make certain they explain their thinking while using academic language. I will begin the lesson reviewing what addition means, and I will have the students explain it in their own words. We will connect this to our new learning of the equal sign. Throughout the lesson, we will discuss how we apply precision and math modeling. This is the mathematical thinking that students will carry with them throughout all grades."

Mr. Scott has used the planning questions to help him plan the curriculum aspect of his lesson. He's decided how his students will have multiple, meaningful opportunities with the learning and how the learning connects to previous and subsequent learning. This will help him then decide *how* they will learn this.

But this planning is about the lesson. Mr. Scott wants to ensure that his students will own this information so he can increase the probability of their learning. He had to determine the following:

▸ How will I share this information with my students?

▸ How will I check that my students understand the goals of the learning?

Mr. Scott tells us that "I always start each day introducing the learning outcome of the lesson. I have a chart that includes *Before*, *Today*, and *Later*. I put today's outcome in the Today box. In the Before box, I include previous learning that connects to today's learning outcome. In this box I will include addition, Attend to Precision, and Model with Mathematics. In the Later box, I will include addition up to twenty, subtraction, Attend to Precision, and Model with Mathematics. Each day, after we discuss today's learning, we discuss how it connects to what we have already learned and where we will continue to use it. With my first graders, it is important that they always have a chance to discuss this with their peers to ensure they understand it. We will also revisit it throughout the lesson."

Mr. Scott knows the importance of his first graders understanding the value of owning their own learning. Thus, he has to answer the following question:

> ▸ How will my students understand that knowing these aspects of the learning support ownership of their learning?

Mr. Scott says, "Every day we reflect on our learning. We talk about the different ways we learned and how we get smarter every day. It is important that my students understand and that they can state the different ways they are learning. We also review what we knew before today and what new thing we learned today. Finally, we discuss what new learning is coming that will help us grow."

Teachers like Mr. Scott realize that without this support—a unit that leads to an authentic demonstration of the learning; a lesson focused on the skill to be learned; opportunities for students to hear about, talk about, read about, and write about their learning; and multiple chances to practice the skill in a variety of situations—his students will struggle with owning their learning.

What Teachers Are Doing

What are other ways teachers have implemented this practice—"Each and every student is supported by **units or lessons** that provide an **integrated approach** and that support **conceptual redundancy** of the learning outcomes"—as they offer support for developing student ownership?

Take this example from a middle school health teacher: "I always include the learning goal from yesterday and tomorrow when I share today's learning goal. In fact, on my board, there is a frame that says, 'Yesterday, Today, and Tomorrow,' and I have the students discuss the connections between them."

Take this example from an elementary school principal: "At our school, the students are expected to always plan with the end in mind. To help solidify this thinking, our teachers decided to display the learning outcomes in the same format: 'Today, I am . . . (the *what*, or the skill of the standard), so that I can . . . (the *why*, or the future use); I will know I am successful when . . . (the *how*, or the product or demonstration).'"

Take this example from a kindergarten teacher: "In order to support my students, I need to understand the scope and sequence of the year so that I can plan backward. Language arts is so recursive, the scope and sequence also let me see when each skill is addressed. Thus, I can plan which lesson is initial instruction, which lessons are for deeper and deeper practice, which lessons are for application, and when the students will be able to transfer this literacy skill into other content areas. Conceptual redundancy also ensures that my students don't forget these skills before they head off to first grade."

Take this example from a high school physics teacher: "As I've spent time understanding my science standards, I've realized that my students need more. The verbs in the standards call for my students to access, analyze, develop, plan, construct, and apply. In order to achieve this level of learning, my students first need to understand the new science concepts, and then they need to be able to apply their learning at a higher level. I was spending too much time lecturing and having students read from text. If they are expected to construct new learning, I knew I had to give them lots of opportunities to work with these new concepts. Now they not only read and hear about them but they must also produce their thinking and learning. This includes talking, writing, modeling, and experimenting. With the integration of these skills, my students are not only more prepared for the level of the standards, but they are retaining the content at a significantly higher level."

What Students Are Saying

What do students say about this practice—"Each and every student is supported by **units or lessons** that provide an **integrated approach** and that support **conceptual redundancy** of the learning outcomes"—and its support for the ownership of their learning?

Take this example from a middle school student: "I know I have time to practice before I have to apply or transfer the skill. This helps me relax while learning—I don't have to be perfect the first time the teacher talks about it."

Take this example from a high school freshman: "Knowing when I am going to apply the skills I am learning has helped me pay closer attention to my work. Before, I would just read along with the teacher, hoping some of the information would stick. We are reading *Romeo and Juliet*, and I will have to argue who changed the most in the play. Because I know how I am going to use the information, I'll take better notes. I don't want to have to reread the whole thing before I begin to write."

Strategic Learning Practice, Curriculum 3

Each and Every Student Is Supported by Access to Curriculum Materials That Match the Content and Rigor of the Learning Outcomes

In order for students to own their learning in regard to curriculum, each and every student must be able to answer the following questions:

▶ What materials am I using to support this learning?

▶ How do these materials support this learning?

▶ What other materials could I use to continue this learning?

In order for teachers to develop students who own their learning in regard to curriculum, it is imperative that teachers support students with practices that are strategically implemented on a daily basis. This requires a focus on those practices that Dusek and Joseph (1985) show increase the opportunities for learning by increasing the opportunities for student ownership. The final Strategic Learning Practice, Curriculum 3, states: "Each and every student is supported by access to **curriculum materials** that match the **content** and **rigor** of the learning outcomes."

Curriculum materials are those student resources that directly support the learning outcomes.

Content is the concept or skill from the standard that is to be learned.

Rigor is the academic level of difficulty of the skill, most often found in the verb of the standard.

The Practice in Action

What does this practice—"Each and every student is supported by access to **curriculum materials** that match the **content** and **rigor** of the learning outcomes"—look like in a classroom at the highest level? You might walk into Ms. Hightower's fifth-grade language arts class and hear her tell her students: "Today, you will determine the theme of a variety of stories, including how characters respond to challenges, in order to complete a character challenges map for each text."

But that is what the teacher said. What happens when you talk with her students and ask them questions?

You: "What are you learning?"

Student: "I am learning to determine the theme of a story, looking specifically at how characters respond to challenges they encounter."

You: "What is theme?"

Student: "Theme is what the book is all about. It is the main idea. Right now I am reading 'The Tortoise and the Hare.' The theme is 'slow and steady wins the race.' That is what the fable is all about."

You: "What other materials are you using to support this learning?"

Student: "Our teacher has picked out a bunch of shorter books and stories. We are practicing completing our character challenges maps. We first have to figure out the theme. Then, we are finding examples of how the characters respond to challenges in the story that connect to the theme. We put these examples on our map. We are using easier books, and some I have already read, so we can have lots of practice."

You: "How do easier books help you as a fifth grader?"

Student: "We won't always use easy books. This is to practice analyzing characters and their responses to challenges. We are going to start reading *The Phantom Tollbooth* this week. That book will be more challenging. But then we will know how to find examples of characters responding to challenges."

You: "What other materials could you use to continue learning about characters and their actions?"

Student: "I guess any good book that has characters responding to challenges. But the character challenges map helps me capture what is happening while I am reading so I can remember how the characters are responding along the way. This will be especially helpful for longer, harder books like *The Phantom Tollbooth*."

Are you wondering how the student was able to answer your questions so clearly and with such confidence? Let's ask Ms. Hightower.

"My students did not answer questions at this level because I simply stated an objective out loud. I had to intentionally plan how I would support my class. First, I needed to know what skill they would learn, what materials I would use to support this learning, how the materials would support the rigor of the learning, and how to ensure the materials would be accessible to everyone. I also had to determine how I would explain at every step of the way what they would be doing."

Ms. Hightower used the Strategic Learning Practice, Curriculum 3, as a frame to help her plan how she wanted to offer this support. This frame is flexible and fits the needs of both teachers and students. However, the following planning questions in table 1.9 helped her focus the support.

Questions to Guide Implementing Strategic Learning Practice, Curriculum 3:

Each and every student is supported by access to curriculum materials that match the content and rigor of the learning outcomes.

Use these planning questions to focus your support.

	Notes
❑ What skill will my students learn, and how will they show they have learned it?	
❑ How do the curriculum materials support the content of the learning outcomes?	
❑ How do the curriculum materials support the rigor of the learning outcomes?	
❑ How will the curriculum materials be accessible to all students?	
❑ How will I share this information with my students?	
❑ How will I check that my students understand the goals of the learning?	
❑ How will my students understand that knowing these aspects of the learning support ownership of their learning?	

Table 1.9: Questions to Guide Implementing Strategic Learning Practice, Curriculum 3

Implementing the Practice

How did Ms. Hightower use the questions in table 1.9 to help plan how she would offer support to her students? First, she had to determine the following:

▶ What skill will my students learn, and how will they show they have learned it?

Ms. Hightower recounts, "I began by reviewing Reading Standard 2 for Literature in English Language Arts at the fifth-grade level: 'Determine a theme of a story, drama, or poem from details in the text, including how characters in a story or drama respond to challenges or how the speaker in a poem reflects upon a topic; summarize the text.'

"I then reviewed the learning progressions for the earlier grades. My students should already know how to determine a theme from details in a text and how to summarize a text. Fifth graders are expected to then be able to determine how characters in a story respond to challenges. I knew that my focus for this lesson was going to be on identifying how characters in a story respond to challenges."

Ms. Hightower then had to determine the answers to the following questions:

▶ How do the curriculum materials support the content of the learning outcomes?

▶ How do the curriculum materials support the rigor of the learning outcomes?

▶ How will the curriculum materials be accessible to all students?

Ms. Hightower continues, "Because I am focused on the standards and not on a reading program, I get to decide what materials I would use to support this skill. Identifying how characters respond to challenges is new for my students. I wanted to choose a text that would allow them to practice and apply this skill. I wanted a text that would be accessible to all learners, regardless of their reading level. I didn't want them struggling through the text. I needed them to use their brain power practicing this new skill without having to deal with the vocabulary and rigor of a difficult text. I chose several short books and texts that would do just that. I even let some students use stories they had read before so they could apply the new skill to it.

"I recognize that curriculum materials also include resources other than text. I needed a strong note-taking template and selected the character challenges map. This will provide students an organized way to gather the specific examples of character responses from the texts. They will be able to apply this resource in future texts as well.

"Once my students are proficient in identifying how characters respond to challenges, they will then apply this skill to *The Phantom Tollbooth*. This is a challenging book for my students. I have an audio version of it as well; my students who will need more support accessing this novel will be provided the opportunity to listen to a chapter before or after reading it."

Ms. Hightower has used the planning questions to help her plan the curriculum aspect of her lesson. She says, "I still haven't decided how I will teach this, but I have decided what materials will support the content and rigor of the outcome."

But this planning is about the lesson. Ms. Hightower wants to ensure that her students will own this information so that she can increase the probability of their learning. She then has to ask herself the following questions:

- ▸ How will I share this information with my students?
- ▸ How will I check that my students understand the goals of the learning?

Ms. Hightower says, "I have a range of reading levels in my classroom this year. It is important that my students, regardless of ability, are all clear on our learning goal for each day. It is equally important that they understand that the materials have been selected to allow each of them to attain the goal. For this reason, I share the plan for the lesson each day with my students. This includes what materials we are using and how these materials will support them. After I share this information, I have the students turn and talk to their shoulder partner to be certain they can explain in their own words our goal, our plan, and how the materials will support them. This is a daily routine in my classroom."

Ms. Hightower is very interested that her fifth graders understand the value of owning their own learning. Thus, she has to determine the following:

- ▸ How will my students understand that knowing these aspects of the learning support ownership of their learning?

Ms. Hightower explains, "I have my students self-assess their progress. The self-assessment includes a reflection on what specific materials best supported their achievements and why. My students are getting stronger in identifying how they are learning and the role their materials play in their progress. They are more confident in requesting materials now that they have found to be most helpful to them."

Teachers like Ms. Hightower have realized that without this support—materials that match the content of the lesson, materials that directly support the learning of the determined skill, and materials that are rigorous and challenge the thinking of the students—her students will struggle with owning their learning.

What Teachers Are Doing

What are other ways teachers have implemented this practice—"Each and every student is supported by access to **curriculum materials** that match the **content** and **rigor** of the learning outcomes"—as they offer support for developing student ownership?

Take this example from an eighth-grade history teacher: "When I think of rigor, I have to look at both the skill and the content—and the time of year. For example, if my students need to learn to cite textual evidence from a primary source, I won't have them jump into the Declaration of Independence immediately. First, I will have them learn how to cite textual evidence from a text everyone knows, maybe even something like 'Goldilocks and the Three Bears.' We will then continue to practice with more challenging texts. I will also be introducing them to primary and secondary sources as texts. By the end of the year, the kids are ready for the Declaration of Independence. I need them to build on their successes."

Take this example from an elementary school teacher: "I used to think that curriculum and materials were the same thing—the math program I was told to use by my district. I never had to think about the standards because I was told that they were covered in my program. With the focus now being on the skills in the standards, I look at materials in a much different way. With my standards-based scope and sequence, I can focus on the standards and skills and choose the best materials to help my students learn. This has freed me up to expand the types of resources my students are exposed to and learn from."

Take this example from a first-grade teacher in science: "Really contemplating what rigor looks like in first grade meant that I had to look more closely at the standards. In the past, I would find the topic and pick a bunch of picture books that related to the topic. But when I look at the standards for first grade, I see that my students must 'make observations to construct an evidence-based account that young plants and animals are like, but not exactly like, their parents.' In order for my students to meet the rigor of this standard, they will have to interact with better materials than just picture books. This opened my eyes to the need of varied resources and other ways to access information—including field trips, videos, and labs."

What Students Are Saying

What do students say about this practice—"Each and every student is supported by access to **curriculum materials** that match the **content** and **rigor** of the learning outcomes"—and its support for the ownership of their learning?

Take this example from a high school senior: "I realized that by the time I got to the last year of high school, I wasn't actually learning anything new in terms of skills. But I was expected to use these skills and apply them to harder and harder texts. This got me ready for college. I know that the skills I have learned in high school are the same as those I will use in college. The increase in rigor has helped me practice for college."

Take this example from a seventh grader in science: "I like how we use technology in this class. In my other classes the teachers would just have us use the computer to do work—but this wasn't challenging to me. In this class, we use a variety of materials to access challenging topics. We get to use the computer to gather research—and we have to figure out if it is factual or not. This is super fun."

Curriculum Reflection

How Well Do You Develop Students to Own What They Are Learning?

In this chapter, we have shown you what student ownership looks like in practice. We have shown you what it sounds like when students own their part in curriculum. And we have given examples of how teachers have implemented these strategic learning practices in a variety of classrooms.

We have also explained the difference between a student who is simply *doing* or *understanding* curriculum and one who is *owning* what they are learning.

Remember we said that a student is *doing* when they can state the task in front of them or recite what they are doing.

Remember we said that a student is *understanding* when they can explain the skill they are learning.

Remember we said that a student is *owning* their learning when they can articulate what skill they are learning, why they are learning it, how they will demonstrate that they have learned it, and how they will use it in the future.

Think of your students. Where do they fall on the doing-understanding-owning continuum? Think about the supports they need from you to develop student ownership. How often and to what degree do you offer these supports? In other words, what impact do you have on student ownership?

John Hattie's research (2011) revealed that "such passion for evaluating impact is the single most critical lever for instructional excellence—accompanied by understanding this impact, and doing something in light of the evidence and understanding" (p. viii).

What follows are reflection activities that will help you determine your impact on student ownership—both areas of strength and areas of growth.

Remember, in order to develop student ownership, all student learning must be driven by a standards-based curriculum with measurable and achievable objectives.

Also remember that your actions are key to the development of student ownership.

Reflect on Strategic Learning Practice, Curriculum 1

Each and every student is supported by relevant standards with measurable and achievable outcomes that are accessible and that drive all learning.

Consider how your students respond to the following questions:

▸ What skill am I learning?

▸ Why am I learning this skill?

▸ How will I know that I have learned this skill?

Think about your students' responses—remembering that your support is directly linked to developing student ownership—and use the following to help you reflect on the strengths and gaps of your support.

How often and how well do you offer these supports?

• The learning outcome aligns with a relevant standard and uses academically appropriate language.

_____

• The learning outcome aligns with what the standard calls for.

_____

• The learning outcome identifies how the students will show the demonstration of the learning.

_____

• All student learning is driven by the learning outcomes and can be attained from the lesson.

_____

• All students have access to the learning outcome.

Table 1.10: Reflect on Strategic Learning Practice, Curriculum 1

Reflect on Strategic Learning Practice, Curriculum 2

Each and every student is supported by units and lessons that provide an integrated approach and that support conceptual redundancy of the learning outcomes.

Consider how your students respond to the following questions:

▸ How does learning in a variety of ways—listening, speaking, reading, and writing—support mastery of the skill?

▸ How does the current learning relate to previous and subsequent learning?

▸ How can I use this learning in the future?

Think about your students' responses—remembering that your support is directly linked to developing student ownership—and use the following to help you reflect on the strengths and gaps of your support.

How often and how well do you offer these supports?

• The unit or lesson integration includes opportunities for students to listen, speak, read, and write about the learning outcome.

_____

• The unit or lesson integration offers students a focus on both the content standards and the learning practices.

_____

• The unit or lesson provides students with conceptual redundancy through multiple, varied interactions with the same concept.

_____

• The unit or lesson aligns with previous learning and builds to subsequent learning.

Table 1.11: Reflect on Strategic Learning Practice, Curriculum 2

Reflect on Strategic Learning Practice, Curriculum 3

Each and every student is supported by access to curriculum materials that match the content and rigor of the learning outcomes.

Consider how your students respond to the following questions:

▸ What materials am I using to support this learning?

▸ How do these materials support this learning?

▸ What other materials could I use to continue this learning?

Think about your students' responses—remembering that your support is directly linked to developing student ownership—and use the following to help you reflect on the strengths and gaps of your support.

How often and how well do you offer these supports?

- The curriculum materials build to mastery of the relevant standards with measurable and achievable learning outcomes.

- The curriculum materials are specifically selected to support the content of the standard or learning outcome.

- The curriculum materials are specifically selected to support the rigor of the standard or learning outcome.

- The curriculum materials are accessible to all students.

Table 1.12: Reflect on Strategic Learning Practice, Curriculum 3

2 INSTRUCTION

Developing Students to Own How They Are Learning

Ask for a definition of the phrase *good teaching*, and you will most likely be answered with an instructional strategy. Good teaching is group work. Good teaching is an entertaining and engaging lecture. Good teaching is direct instruction. Good teaching is inquiry method or complex instruction or scaffolding or differentiated instruction. Most people associate teaching with some form of methodology. Thus, most teachers think about their lessons through the lens of instruction.

But this approach to instruction focuses on the teacher—what they need to do to teach the skills. We want to flip this focus onto the students—what *they* need to do to learn the skills. True student ownership begins when the teacher looks at instruction from the students' point of view.

[handwritten margin note: Good teaching]

Instruction is defined as those strategies students will use to master the content and skills determined in curriculum. That is, once the student understands what they are learning, how they will show mastery, and why they are learning it, they must then determine the best way to learn. This is done with the support of the teacher. Madeline Hunter (1982) explains that "teaching is now defined as a constant stream of professional decisions made before, during, and after interactions with students; decisions which, when implemented, increase the probability of learning" (p. 3). The decisions that best support student learning also best support student ownership.

The Imperatives for Ownership of Instruction

To develop student ownership, several things are imperative: It is imperative for students to know and be able to articulate how they will learn the skills they are mastering in the day's lesson, in the unit, and in the course. It is imperative for students to understand how the instructional strategies they are using effectively support them to master these skills. It is imperative that they know and are able to articulate which strategies support their learning and how to apply them during the current class, in other classes, and when they are working on their own. It is imperative that they understand the value of pushing their learning by listening, speaking, reading, and writing with colleagues. It is imperative that they understand their role in their own learning—that they are the masters of their own mastery.

Table 2.1 provides some helpful indicators that reveal when students are taking ownership of their learning.

How Do Students Demonstrate Ownership of Instruction?

Each and every student is able to articulate:

- what they are learning and how they will demonstrate they have learned it,
- how they are learning,
- how engaging in conversations with their peers pushes their own learning,
- how they participate in these conversations,
- how their role as both a speaker and a listener supports their learning,
- how the instructional strategy they are using effectively supports them to master the learning,
- how they can utilize this strategy in future learning,
- the value of reflecting on how they learn,
- why the allotted time is provided,
- how best to utilize that time to support their learning,
- how routines can help them in the future, and
- why articulating these aspects of instruction helps them own their learning.

Table 2.1: Indicators of Student Ownership of Instruction

If students are able to articulate the points in table 2.1 effectively, they are engaging in the process of metacognition. Metacognition is a learner's ability to think about their own thinking, to know what they are knowing, and to learn about their own learning—in other words, metacognition is cognition about cognition. Allen Newell (1990) identifies two aspects of metacognition: (1) knowledge about cognition and (2) regulation of cognition. Thus, the strongest strategies we can engage in with our students are those that teach them about their learning and that can be applied to push their learning in other situations. This also leads to greater student ownership.

Putting Student Ownership into Practice

But what does student ownership look like in practice? What does it sound like when a student owns their part in instruction? What is the difference between a student who is simply *doing* or *understanding* instruction and one who is *owning* how they are learning?

A student is *doing* when they can state how they need to complete the task in front of them.

A student is *understanding* when they can explain what strategy they are engaged in.

A student is *owning* how they are learning when they can articulate the strategy they are currently using to learn, how this strategy supports their learning, and how they will use this strategy in the future—during this class, in other classes, and when they are working on their own.

The tables that follow—table 2.2, table 2.3, table 2.4, and table 2.5—present some examples of what this looks and sounds like on a continuum of doing-understanding-owning in a variety of content areas and grade levels, particularly when we ask the question, "How are you learning this?"

Possible responses on the continuum from first grade students in math when asked,

"How are you learning?"

"I have to make a picture of each number."

"I am working with my elbow partner. We are making models of our addition problems. Then we write them using numbers."

"We learned that the numbers on both sides of the equal sign must be the same. You can't use an equal sign if this is not true. Today we have to tell each other if the problem is true or false. Then we make a model with blocks to show if it is true. If it is true, our model shows this. If it is false, we have to fix it."

DOING   UNDERSTANDING   OWNING

Table 2.2: Student Ownership Continuum, Math, Grade 1

Possible responses on the continuum from fourth grade students in English-language arts when asked,

"How are you learning?"

"When asked, I have to tell who the narrator of the story is."

"We are using Cornell notes to determine the narrator of the story and then find words from the story that we can use as evidence."

"We are learning about point of view and the difference between first-person and third-person. We are using Cornell notes to gather how different authors use different ways to show who is narrating. Cornell notes help me keep track of the evidence from the text without having to write down every single word. I take notes this way in my other classes. It helps organize my thoughts."

DOING   UNDERSTANDING   OWNING

Table 2.3: Student Ownership Continuum, English-Language Arts, Grade 4

Possible responses on the continuum from eighth grade
students in physical science when asked,

"How are you learning?"

"I am
drawing a
picture of a
molecule to show
protons and
neutrons."

"We are
making models
to show examples of
simple molecules and
extended structures.
We will include
protons and
neutrons."

"We use
models to helps us
understand and describe
things, especially things that we
can't see, like simple molecules and
extended structure. We are going
to make models of them so we can
understand and explain them better. Not
only will I learn more from making my
models, but when I see everyone else's
models, I will understand even better.
My teacher suggests I use this
strategy in other classes,
like Math."

DOING   **UNDERSTANDING**   **OWNING**

Table 2.4: Student Ownership Continuum, Physical Science, Grade 8

Possible responses on the continuum from high school
students in American history when asked,

"How are you learning?"

"I have to list
three causes of
World War I in
my notebook."

"We are using a
point of view chart
to clarify why different
countries entered World
War I. I will listen to the
teacher's lecture and
take notes."

"We are
learning about
points of view. Today we are
reading about World War I and
why each country entered it. We are
gathering information on a point of view
chart. In our groups, each of us represents
the point of view of a different country.
Before we can discuss their reason, we
must understand it from their point of
view. We come to consensus before
we take notes on our chart. This
means we must negotiate
our answers."

DOING   **UNDERSTANDING**   **OWNING**

Table 2.5: Student Ownership Continuum, American History, High School

Moving to Student Ownership

What can a teacher do to move a student toward owning their learning? Student ownership is best defined as a mindset. Students who know they have the authority, capacity, and responsibility to own their learning possess an ownership mindset. Thus, to move students, the teacher must delegate the authority, build the capacity, and give the responsibility to each and every student.

How does a teacher do this? They must model the thinking behind the ownership and explicitly teach the skills of ownership. This takes planning. In order for students to answer the questions posed earlier—"How will I learn this?", "How will this strategy help me learn this?", and "How can I use this strategy in the future and in different situations?"—teachers must be strategic in the practices they use to increase learning.

While there are hundreds of actions a teacher must take in a day, we will focus on those three practices in instruction that research shows increase the opportunities for learning—by increasing the opportunities for student ownership.

Teachers must strategically decide when to offer the following three learning practices:

- **Strategic Learning Practice, Instruction 1:** Each and every student is supported by opportunities for meaningful engagement using structured student-to-student communication.

- **Strategic Learning Practice, Instruction 2:** Each and every student is supported by opportunities for meaningful engagement using effective instructional strategies.

- **Strategic Learning Practice, Instruction 3:** Each and every student is supported by opportunities for meaningful engagement in which instructional time is used efficiently.

In the following sections, we will clearly define each learning practice, describe what implementation looks and sounds like in the classroom, share teacher planning questions, offer examples of how students have been supported with these learning practices in a variety of content areas and grade levels, and explain how these practices directly lead to increased student ownership.

Strategic Learning Practice, Instruction 1

Each and Every Student Is Supported by Opportunities for Meaningful Engagement Using Structured Student-to-Student Communication

In order for students to own their learning in regard to instruction, each and every student must be able to answer the following questions:

▸ How does engaging in conversations with my peers push my learning?

▸ How do I participate in these conversations? *–productively.*

▸ What is my role as both a speaker and a listener?

In order for teachers to develop students who own their learning in regard to instruction, it is imperative that they support them with practices that are strategically implemented on a daily basis. This requires a focus on those practices that Duzinski (1987) and Rosenshine and Meister (1994) show increase the opportunities for learning by increasing the opportunities for student ownership. Strategic Learning Practice, Instruction 1, states: "Each and every student is supported by **opportunities** for **meaningful engagement** using **structured student-to-student communication**."

First, let's define each aspect of this practice.

Opportunities are those chances for students to be actively engaged. The greater the quantity and the higher the quality of these opportunities, the higher the probability of student learning.

Meaningful engagement happens in those times when students are involved in interactions that directly lead to increased understanding or mastery of the learning outcome.

Structured implies that these interactions have a purpose, a value, and a goal. These interactions can be planned by the teacher or the students, but everyone should be clear on their role in the interaction.

Student-to-student communication is an interaction between students in which each has an opportunity to push their thinking and understanding of the learning through speaking and listening.

The Practice in Action

What does this practice—"Each and every student is supported by **opportunities** for **meaningful engagement** using **structured student-to-student communication**"—look like in a classroom at the highest level? You might walk into Mrs. Rodriguez's second-grade class during science and read the following learning outcome on the flip chart: "We will make observations to construct an evidence-based account of how an object made of a small set of pieces can be disassembled and made into a new object by accurately completing the Melting Objects lab report."

2nd grade?

That is what the students read, but what happens when you ask them questions about their learning?

You: "What are you learning?"

Student: "I am learning about how objects can change. Today my group is experimenting with how objects can change from solids to liquids. We have to gather evidence to show our learning."

You: "I see you are working with and talking to other students during the experiment. How does this help you?"

Student: "First, it helps me because we get to help one another. We all have jobs in our group. I am in charge of recording our evidence today. We have to record what we see—we use the word *observe*. We will also weigh our objects before and after to see if the weight changed. We need to put that data in too. But before we write anything, we have to talk about it with our group to make sure it is all right. But it also helps us because we get to talk about and ask questions about what we are learning. Mrs. Rodriguez tells us we have to make our thinking out loud. We have to share ideas and listen to others. We all get smarter that way."

You: "How do you know what to talk about?"

Student: "We can talk about anything that will help us with the experiment, but we have to make sure we talk about the things the teacher puts on our sentence frames."

You: "What is a sentence frame?"

Student: "It gives us a question to ask, and the frame tells us how to answer it. We have to use the new words we have been learning in our answer. And we have to answer in a complete sentence. It gives us practice with the new things we are learning about."

Are you wondering how the student was able to answer your questions so clearly and with such confidence? Let's ask Mrs. Rodriguez.

"I have been working a lot with my students to make sure they understand everything we are learning and how talking is critical to their education. The objective you see on the chart is just the beginning. It is the planning that has really supported them. I am very deliberate in making certain they know why engaging with peers will push their learning. I also have to continually model how to participate in a conversation and model their role as both a speaker and a listener."

Mrs. Rodriguez used the Strategic Learning Practice, Instruction 1, as a frame to help her plan how she wanted to offer this support. This frame is flexible and fits the needs of both teachers and students. However, the following planning questions in table 2.6 helped her focus the support.

Questions to Guide Implementing Strategic Learning Practice, Instruction 1:

Each and every student is supported by opportunities for meaningful engagement using structured student-to-student communication.

Use these planning questions to focus your support.

	Notes
❑ What skill will my students learn, and how will they demonstrate they have learned it?	
❑ How will I provide multiple, varied opportunities for student communication?	
❑ How do student communications build toward mastery of the learning outcome?	
❑ How do student communications provide high-quality reciprocal speaking and listening opportunities?	
❑ How will I share this information with my students?	
❑ How will I check that my students understand the goals of the conversation?	
❑ How will my students understand that reflecting on the instructional aspects of the learning supports ownership of their learning?	

Table 2.6: Questions to Guide Implementing Strategic Learning Practice, Instruction 1

Implementing the Practice

How did Mrs. Rodriguez use the questions in table 2.6 to help plan how she would offer support to her students? First, she had to determine the following:

▸ What skill will my students learn, and how will they demonstrate they have learned it?

Mrs. Rodriguez begins by explaining, "We are in a physical science unit on structure and properties of matter. The performance expectation for 2-PS1-3 is: 'Make observations to construct an evidence-based account of how an object made of a small set of pieces can be disassembled and made into a new object.' In first grade, the students began making science observations and constructing evidence. I wanted to build on these skills but with a focus on structures and properties of matter as they explored how a small set of pieces can be disassembled and made into a new object.

"I knew I had a lot to focus on with this lesson. I needed to deepen their understanding of the concept of changing matter, I needed to reinforce making observations to construct an evidence-based account, and I needed to support the continued development of academic language. I knew my students would need to work together and talk a lot if they were going to be successful."

With the first guiding question to implementing Strategic Learning Practice, Instruction 1, completed, Mrs. Rodriguez next had to determine the following:

▸ How will I provide multiple, varied opportunities for student communication?

▸ How do student communications build toward mastery of the learning outcome?

▸ How do student communications provide high-quality reciprocal speaking and listening opportunities?

Mrs. Rodriguez continues, "I had to decide when, why, and how my students would talk. Every lesson begins with an overview of the unit goal and the daily objective. This is a routine in my class. We review them, and students talk with their shoulder partner to make certain they understand what we are learning today and where our learning is going.

"For this lesson, I wanted to begin by reviewing what we have learned so far about the properties of matter. It is important that my students talk with lots of other students, not just their shoulder partner or their friends. I use an appointment clock in my classroom. This not only reinforces telling time but also lets my students get up and talk to other students. I had the students meet with their twelve o'clock appointment to review what we have learned so far. The students had to share out one item their partner shared with them. This requires them to be good listeners.

"When I got students into their experiment groups, I wanted to make sure they were talking every step of the way. But I also wanted to make certain their conversations were focused, pushed the skills we are learning about, and were in complete sentences. I used sentence frames for this. Each group has a set of questions and answer sentence frames that they must complete throughout the experiment.

"For example, in this experiment they need to answer the question: 'How did the object change?' They can answer this using the sentence frame: 'One way the object changed was _____. My evidence of this change is _____.'

"The next question asks: 'What is one way the object did not change?' The answer frames read: 'One way the object did not change was _____. My evidence to support this is _____.' These frames have helped my students have more focused, meaningful conversations that push their learning—while using academic language at the same time."

But Mrs. Rodriguez wanted to ensure that her students would be able to use the skills in a variety of situations. She wanted to help her students own this information so that she could increase the probability of their learning. Therefore, she then had to ask herself the following questions:

▸ How will I share this information with my students?

▸ How will I check that my students understand the goals of the conversation?

Mrs. Rodriguez says, "We have discussed the role of speaking and listening for learning from day one in our classroom. My students will tell you that they have to share ideas and listen to others. We will all get smarter that way. Throughout the lesson, we discuss what we have talked about. We specifically discuss how the conversations helped us. This can mean it confirmed what we knew, it stretched our learning, or it made us think differently.

"In today's lesson, I reviewed the questions and sentence frames before the experiment. It was important to me that the students knew what they were going to talk about and why."

Mrs. Rodriguez was very interested in helping her second graders understand the value of owning their own learning. Thus, she had to determine the following:

> ▸ How will my students understand that reflecting on the
>   instructional aspects of the learning supports ownership of
>   their learning?

Mrs. Rodriguez observes, "Every day we talk about our learning. We share what conversations we had about our learning. We share how the conversations confirmed what we knew, stretched what we were learning, or made us think differently. When the students share, it is not just about the skill or concept. We reflect on how the talking and listening specifically helped us learn more. It's funny, I was out one day and had a substitute teacher. The students told me it was hard to learn that day because the classroom was so quiet. They understand the value of conversation for learning."

Teachers like Mrs. Rodriguez have realized that without this support—multiple opportunities to make meaning by sharing with other learners, speaking and listening about the learning, and building on one another's thoughts and ideas—her students would struggle with owning their learning.

What Teachers Are Doing

What are other ways teachers have implemented this practice—"Each and every student is supported by **opportunities** for **meaningful engagement** using **structured student-to-student communication**"—as they offer support for developing student ownership?

Take this example from a high school science teacher: "My students have really benefited from my learning more about structured communication. This used to be one of my weaknesses. I had always pictured the 'think, pair, share' as a silly activity until I saw a colleague effectively implementing it. I went back and tried it in my classroom and was surprised at how successful it was. I love that it gets all students talking, even the ones I didn't think would be active participators. I also needed a way to get all my students to be more comfortable with sharing with the whole class. This is what I tried: My students sit at lab tables in groups of four. Each seat has a colored sticker, and when I have students talk, I draw a colored pom-pom out of a cup, and the person in the corresponding colored seat completes the task. Sometimes I have more than one person at the table reciprocally share—one person reads something aloud to the table, one person shares the answer to a question, and another person agrees or disagrees. I also tell students that I will use a random number generator to call on a student, but I give the table time to discuss before I select the person. There are so many great ways to get students talking, but I was never comfortable employing the strategy before. Now it is one of the most effective things I do. Whenever a class seems dead and isn't participating, I know I can count on using structured communication to facilitate discussion. This works in all levels of my classes, from regular to AP. My student teacher and I were just having a conversation on how drastically the energy and participation in a room can change when we start using colored pom-poms!"

Take this example from a junior high school health teacher: "My kids love to talk, but they wouldn't stay on task. I realized that it was because my questions weren't 'meaty' enough, and the students didn't need that much time to answer them. After attending a PD session on DOK levels, I began having the kids answer more thoughtful questions. They are much more interested in staying on task because the conversation is making them think."

Take this example from a fourth-grade teacher: "After I introduced the social studies vocabulary, I had students using the words every day with each other. During these conversations they had a chance to say the words and hear the words many times. When they took the quiz on Friday, everyone passed!"

Take this example from a second-grade math teacher: "I have my students turn and talk at every transition in the lesson. I have them remind one another of the learning intention and the success criteria. This helps them stay on track and gives me a chance to check for understanding."

Take this example from a high school principal: "My teachers have always asked good questions. They just never waited for the students to answer. They were impatient and would call on the one student who raised their hand and move on. When they realized that students needed to talk, and they gave them the time, they saw that the students were more engaged. But it's been a struggle to get them to give students the time."

What Students Are Saying

What do students say about this practice—"Each and every student is supported by **opportunities** for **meaningful engagement** using **structured student-to-student communication**"—and its support for the ownership of their learning?

Take this example from a fifth grader: "Talking helps me understand my thinking. Sometimes I know what I am thinking, but when I try to explain it, it doesn't make any sense. Telling someone else helps me figure out my ideas. And listening helps me understand what other kids are thinking."

Take this example from a middle school student: "Sometimes when the teacher is talking, I don't understand. But when we get to talk to one another, that helps. Other students can explain it in a way that makes sense to me."

Take this example from a junior in high school: "My government teacher gives interesting lectures. Before he'd just talk the entire time, and I got most of it, I think. But lately he has given us time about every ten minutes to chat with each other to make sure we got the most important details of the lecture. This has helped me a lot. My notes are much more complete, and I feel that I understand the content better."

Strategic Learning Practice, Instruction 2

Each and Every Student Is Supported by Opportunities for Meaningful Engagement Using Effective Instructional Strategies

In order for students to own their learning in regard to instruction, each and every student must be able to answer the following questions:

▸ How does engaging in this instructional strategy support my learning?

▸ How can I use this instructional strategy in the future?

▸ What is the value of reflecting on my learning?

In order for teachers to develop students who own their learning in regard to instruction, it is imperative that teachers support students with practices that are strategically implemented on a daily basis. This requires a focus on those practices that Marzano (1998), Seidel and Shavelson (2007), Swanson and Hoskyn (1998), Fendick (1990), and Walker, Greenwood, Hart, and Carta (1994) show increase the opportunities for learning by increasing the opportunities for student ownership. Strategic Learning Practice, Instruction 2, states: "Each and every student is supported by **opportunities** for **meaningful engagement** using **effective instructional strategies**."

First, let's define each aspect of this practice.

Opportunities are those chances for students to be actively engaged. The greater the quantity and the higher the quality of these opportunities, the higher the probability of student learning.

Meaningful engagement happens in those times when students are participating in interactions that directly lead to increased understanding or mastery of the learning outcome.

Effective implies that the students demonstrate the intended learning at the end of the time allotted.

Instructional strategies are all of the approaches a teacher may employ to engage their students in learning that meets the determined objective and outcome of the unit or lesson. These instructional strategies take into account both the skill to be learned and the students learning the skill.

The Practice in Action

What does this practice—"Each and every student is supported by **opportunities** for **meaningful engagement** using **effective instructional strategies**"—look like in a classroom at the highest level? You might walk into Mr. Spicer's eighth-grade language arts class, and on the first page of the class agenda, found in the students' Chromebook, you will read: "Unit Standard: Analyze how a text—*Narrative of the Life of Frederick Douglass, an American Slave*, by Frederick Douglass—makes connections among and distinctions between individuals, ideas, or events (e.g., through comparisons, analogies, or categories). Unit Outcome: Write an explanatory and informative essay that compares the life of a slave to that of his master. Lesson Outcome: Analyze how chapters 5–7 make connections among and distinctions between Frederick Douglass and Mr. Auld in order to cite specific textual evidence with Cornell notes. You will read the text in your reciprocal teaching talk groups."

This agenda shows a well-planned unit by Mr. Spicer. But what happens when you ask students about their learning? How much do they own of the process? The students are sitting in groups as you walk around.

You: "What are you learning?"

Deb: "We're learning how to analyze a text on Frederick Douglass and how it compares and contrasts."

Zach: "The standard uses the phrase *makes connections among and distinctions between individuals.*"

Deb: "Oh yeah. Mr. Spicer tells us to use as much academic language as we can. But we need to read the text and then find accurate evidence we can use in our essays."

You: "How will you read the text? Is that why you are sitting in groups?"

Zach: "Yes, we're in our reciprocal teaching talk groups, and we will read the text together, discuss it, make sure we have all understood it, and then take notes."

Deb: "We each have a role. Today I will be the questioner, Zach will be the clarifier, Jamal will be the summarizer, and Jane will be the predictor. As the questioner, I will read the paragraph out loud to the group. I will then ask them a couple of questions—one that is explicit and can be answered with words from the text and another that is more inferential and can be answered by putting ideas together that might not be explicitly stated."

Zach: "Then I will clarify any vocabulary or phrases that the group is struggling with. We will also find the vocabulary Mr. Spicer told us we need to know about slavery and abolition. After I clarify, Jamal will summarize what we read, and we will add to it if we need to. Then Jane will make a prediction about what we will read about next. She will use words from what we just read or any text features—like titles and subheadings and captions—to make this prediction. We will agree or disagree and add our evidence."

Deb: "Before we move on to the next section, we will take notes using Cornell notes. We will check with one another that they are accurate and then read the next section."

You: "How does this help you learn?"

Jamal: "Reciprocal teaching helps me learn because it makes me read and reread the text. By having to answer the questions, clarify vocabulary and ideas, summarize, and then predict, I am understanding at a deeper level. If I read this by myself, I might think I know it all without realizing what I missed."

Jane: "I like these groups because it is fun to talk and find out what others are thinking. I also like the roles because this is what I need to be doing in my own head when I read by myself. The group lets me practice and see how others do it."

You: "How did you learn to do reciprocal teaching?"

Deb: "Mr. Spicer taught us about each skill individually at the beginning of the year. So, we spent a lot of time developing questions, clarifying vocabulary, summarizing, and using text clues to predict. We then got into groups and began practicing putting the skills together."

Zach: "Because it is toward the end of the year, Mr. Spicer is having us do as much of this work on our own as possible. We can ask him for help but only after we have all asked one another first. He says this is what will be expected of us in high school."

Are you wondering how Deb, Zach, Jamal, and Jane were able to answer your questions so articulately and with such confidence? Let's ask Mr. Spicer.

"First off, I had to make sure they understood what we were learning—in both the unit and the lesson. Then I had to determine the best way to have them learn this—there are so many strategies to choose from. Reciprocal teaching is an instructional strategy that we have been using all year, so the students are very familiar with it. We have used it in a lot of different contexts and with a lot of support from me, but this is the first time I have asked them to work in talk groups where they are in control of everything—the roles, the chunking of the text, time management. To do this I need to be very planned. I also need to be very deliberate about what we are learning and where we are headed—what we will complete at the end of the lesson and unit."

Mr. Spicer used the Strategic Learning Practice, Instruction 2, as a frame to help him plan how he wanted to offer this support. This frame is flexible and fits the needs of both teachers and students. However, the following planning questions in table 2.7 helped him focus the support.

Questions to Guide Implementing Strategic Learning Practice, Instruction 2:

Each and every student is supported by opportunities for meaningful engagement using effective instructional strategies.

Use these planning questions to focus your support.

	Notes
❑ What skill will my students learn, and how will they demonstrate they have learned it?	
❑ How will I select an instructional strategy that will build toward mastery of the learning outcome?	
❑ How will I select an instructional strategy that is appropriate for my students?	
❑ How does the instructional strategy require a high level of active participation?	
❑ How will I share this information with my students?	
❑ How will I check that my students understand the goals of the instruction?	
❑ How will my students understand that reflecting on the instructional aspects of the learning supports ownership of their learning?	

Table 2.7: Questions to Guide Implementing Strategic Learning Practice, Instruction 2

Implementing the Practice

How did Mr. Spicer use the questions in table 2.7 to help plan how he would offer support to his students? First, he had to ask himself the following question:

▸ What skill will my students learn, and how will they demonstrate they have learned it?

Mr. Spicer observes, "We are at the end of the year, and my students still need a lot of practice reading informational texts. In social studies, my students are learning about the Civil War, so the narrative by Frederick Douglass fits in nicely. I selected the standard 8.RI.3: 'Analyze how a text makes connections among and distinctions between individuals, ideas, or events (e.g., through comparisons, analogies, or categories).' This standard helped me determine the focus for the end-of-unit essay. After that, the curriculum side of planning this unit came fairly quickly."

Mr. Spicer then had to determine the answers to the following questions:

▸ How will I select an instructional strategy that will build toward mastery of the learning outcome?

▸ How will I select an instructional strategy that is appropriate for my students?

▸ How does the instructional strategy require a high level of active participation?

Mr. Spicer says, "I realized that the unit and the final essay hinged on the students' ability to comprehend a fairly complex text. Frederick Douglass wrote this narrative in 1845 using his particular vernacular. I knew there would be vocabulary and ideas that were new to my students. I also knew that they needed to grapple with the text and its concepts if they were to pull relevant evidence from it to use in their essays. And, as it was the end of the year, they needed to practice working independently to get ready for high school.

"That's why my first decision was how they were to access the text. Of all the strategies I could choose from—close reading, teacher-led lectures, readings for homework driven by end-of-chapter quizzes, direct instruction, and so on—it became clear that reciprocal teaching talk groups would lead to the strongest outcome. Why? Because first it would lead to mastery of both the unit and lesson objective. The thinking required to question, clarify, summarize, and predict about specific passages in a text really pushes students' deeper understanding of the content. So, I knew that this was a strong strategy.

"Next, I had to determine if it was appropriate for my students. The maturity of an eighth grader is different for each student. But I knew my students needed to begin working more independently, especially from me. Again, reciprocal teaching seemed to fit the bill. My students had been practicing each of the strategies for the entire year—I had them learning in groups since November—and they had been working on the social skills necessary to be effective as a learning team. For the majority of my class, they were up to the task. And the smaller groups I had them in let me monitor and manage those teams that needed the extra support.

"I also knew that the instructional strategy I selected needed to require a high level of active participation for each student. The individual roles in reciprocal teaching ensured this. And the students would hold one another accountable to participate."

Mr. Spicer also wanted to ensure that his students would be able to use these skills in a variety of situations—especially in high school. He wanted his students to own these strategies so they could increase the probability of their learning. He then had to determine the following:

▸ How will I share this information with my students?

▸ How will I check that my students understand the goals of the instruction?

Mr. Spicer explains, "We have focused on reading strategies from the beginning of the year. We discussed the value of having a variety of reading strategies at their disposal when reading anything—novels, poems, newspaper articles, biographies, the textbook, and so on. We discussed the need to learn and practice many different strategies to find out which ones work best for them. We discussed how the skills of reciprocal teaching—questioning, clarifying, summarizing, and predicting—form a nice schema to help categorize these strategies. And we discussed how the format of reciprocal teaching—working in small groups to make meaning—forms a nice process to help them understand how to learn from one another.

"Reciprocal teaching forces the cognitive load onto my students, which allows me to spend my time supporting the instruction. The small groups help me check for understanding, clarify any concerns, support the process of reading, support the process of gathering evidence, and differentiate for individual teams, as needed."

Mr. Spicer wanted his students to understand the value of owning their learning. He wanted to prepare them for high school and college. Therefore, he needed to think about the following question:

▸ How will my students understand that reflecting on the instructional aspects of the learning supports ownership of their learning?

Mr. Spicer says, "We have had many discussions about the value of making meaning from text and understanding how a reader goes about making meaning. For each new reading strategy, we discuss what it is, how to use it, how it can help a reader understand at a deeper level, and how to employ it in a variety of situations. My students are expected to use these strategies in other classes and report out how they have helped them."

Teachers like Mr. Spicer have realized that without this support—multiple opportunities to actively engage in the learning, interacting with instruction that is purposeful and leads to mastery and a deeper understanding of the learning, and reflecting on the use of these strategies in the future —his students will struggle with owning their learning.

What Teachers Are Doing

What are other ways teachers have implemented this practice—"Each and every student is supported by **opportunities** for **meaningful engagement** using **effective instructional strategies**"—as they offer support for developing student ownership?

Take this example from a sixth-grade language arts teacher: "I love going to professional development on instructional strategies—the more ideas I have, the better. I used to learn something new, and then I'd come back to class and use it until I got tired of it. However, I didn't spend as much time thinking about the learning outcome of the lesson or the needs of my students. I thought everything had to do with instruction. I now realize that while instruction is key, I can't make an effective decision about which strategy to use until I have determined the skill to be learned in the lesson and the outcome that shows mastery. Once I have decided these, I can then figure out the best method for my students to learn that skill and produce that outcome."

Take this example from a high school mathematics teacher: "We learn a lot of procedures in our classes. I found that many of my students were just following the steps but not thinking about the math or their learning. This led to students who would encounter a challenging problem and immediately give up and say, 'I don't know how to do this one.' I knew I had to do a better job building their metacognition. We began to talk out loud as we solved problems. We would say what we already knew about the problem, what patterns we saw from previous problems, what the problem asked for, and what would be our first approach and why. We questioned one another and made our thinking visible. Talking about our thinking publicly helped my students understand the strategies they were employing and the decisions behind them. Not only has their math improved, but, equally important, their confidence has also improved."

Take this example from a primary teacher: "I tend to use direct instruction when my students are learning their basic decoding skills. Once they are able to decode but need to practice their comprehension, I tend to use close reading strategies. I use whichever strategy makes the most sense for the skill to be learned."

Take this example from an elementary science teacher: "I love teaching science and always have done a lot of experiments with my students. When I learned more about the new science standards, I realized I couldn't just have my students observe experiments if I wanted them to meet the standards. I needed my students to actively seek solutions, design investigations, and ask new questions. I needed to understand and utilize the method of inquiry. I also needed to be sure my students understood the difference and why it would help them. They were now going to have to think more like scientists and problem solve, use a variety of tools, collect and analyze information, synthesize information, and so on. I had to shift my strategies from what I have always done to what would help my students meet the standards."

Take this example from a high school psychology teacher: "For me, instruction is all about metacognition. I want my students to understand how they learn, what helps them and why, and what seems to hinder them and why.

I also want them to determine ways to utilize these strategies in a variety of educational settings. I have my students reflect on their learning and learning strategies every day."

What Students Are Saying

What do students say about this practice—"Each and every student is supported by **opportunities** for **meaningful engagement** using **effective instructional strategies**"—and its support for the ownership of their learning?

Take this example from a third grader: "When we are learning how to do something new in math, my teacher always shows us what it looks like first. We then do it together as an entire class. She has us work in pairs to practice even more. Finally, she has us try it on our own to see if we have learned it for ourselves. If not, she gives us more time to practice. This way of learning helps me, especially in math when I have to learn steps."

Take this example from a middle school student: "My teacher tells us each day our plan for learning. She lets us know why she chose what she chose. I can usually see why it makes sense. When we are learning something new, she does a lot of modeling and explaining. When we are practicing something, we usually do it with a partner so we can talk about what we are doing and how it is going. One day our teacher told us we were going to work in groups to read the next chapters. Some of us asked if we could read them on our own and had to tell her why. She let us because she said we understood how we learned best. I understand better now how I need to do things differently sometimes in order to get to the end goal."

We do this!

Strategic Learning Practice, Instruction 3

Each and Every Student Is Supported by Opportunities for Meaningful Engagement in Which Instructional Time Is Used Efficiently

In order for students to own their learning in regard to instruction, each and every student must be able to answer the following questions:

- How much time do I have to learn this?
- How can I use my time most efficiently?
- How can these routines help me in the future?

In order for teachers to develop students who own their learning in regard to instruction, it is imperative that teachers support students with practices that are strategically implemented on a daily basis. This requires a focus on those practices that Kumar (1991) and Datta and Narayanan (1989) show increase the opportunities for learning by increasing the opportunities for student ownership. Our final Strategic Learning Practice, Instruction 3, states: "Each and every student is supported by **opportunities** for **meaningful engagement** in which **instructional time** is used **efficiently**."

First, let's define each aspect of this practice.

Opportunities are chances for students to be actively engaged. The greater the quantity and the higher the quality of these opportunities, the higher the probability of student learning.

Meaningful engagement happens in times when students participate in interactions that directly lead to increased understanding or mastery of the learning outcome.

Instructional time is the time allotted by the teacher for the unit or lesson. Once the unit or lesson begins, this time can become flexible to the needs of the learners.

Efficiently refers to the least amount of time required for the highest rate of learning. Nonproductive time is kept to a minimum.

The Practice in Action

What does this practice—"Each and every student is supported by **opportunities** for **meaningful engagement** in which **instructional time** is used **efficiently**"—look like in a classroom at the highest level? You might walk into Mr. Lee's geometry class and hear his class discussing the following learning outcome: "Students will draw and justify a geometric figure given a rotation, reflection, and translation by accurately utilizing transformation software to complete the activity."

That is what the students discussed. But what happens when you ask individual students about their learning?

You: "What are you learning?"

Student: "I am learning about rotations, reflections, and translations of geometric figures. We have been learning about each one throughout the week. Today we are doing all three to make certain we understand each one. We will need to draw the accurate transformations on trace paper and then on the math software. We also need to be able to justify why our drawings are accurate."

You: "When I first came into the classroom everyone was doing a paired activity. I noticed everyone ended the activity and went straight to discussing the learning outcome as a class. How did you all know to end the activity?"

Student: "Mr. Lee has a timer on the screen. Every day when we come into the room we have a warm-up activity. Sometimes we do it alone, sometimes with a partner. But we only have a set amount of time. When the timer ends, we stop."

You: "How does the timer help you?"

Student: "It is a quick activity, but sometimes at the beginning of class, it is easy to get distracted. The timer helps me know I have to get going right away. And we know each class will start this way. It is how we do things in Mr. Lee's class."

You: "How did you know who was going to be your partner today?"

Student: "At the beginning of the year, Mr. Lee assigned us partners. Now at the beginning of each week, we choose our own partner. If someone doesn't have a partner today, we add them to our group. We can't waste time trying to figure out who to talk to."

You: "I noticed that you are using your notebook during the lesson. How does your notebook help you?"

Student: "When we learn something new, we have to take really good notes. We know we have to refer to our notes first if we have a question, and then we can talk to a classmate. Only after that can we ask Mr. Lee. I try to do this now in all of my classes—take good notes, that is. It helps me find the answers when I get lost.

"One of the things I like best about Mr. Lee's class is that he has taught me to be more organized with my time. His routines have helped me save time in other classes—even if no one else is doing them."

Are you wondering how the student was able to answer your questions with such confidence? Let's find out from Mr. Lee.

"There are a lot of new skills in the geometry curriculum. I know that I do not have any time to waste. It is important to me that my class runs bell to bell. In order for this to happen, I need tight routines and a well-planned lesson. This takes a bit longer to establish at the beginning of the year, but once it is in place we can move at a good pace and focus on the skills and learning."

Mr. Lee used the Strategic Learning Practice, Instruction 3, as a frame to help him plan how he wanted to offer this support. This frame is flexible and fits the needs of both teachers and students. However, the following planning questions in table 2.8 helped him focus the support.

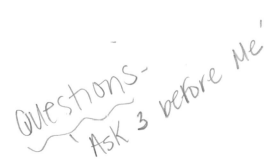

Questions to Guide Implementing Strategic Learning Practice, Instruction 3:

Each and every student is supported by opportunities for meaningful engagement in which instructional time is used efficiently.

Use these planning questions to focus your support.

	Notes
❑ What skill will my students learn, and how will they demonstrate they have learned it?	
❑ How much time will I allot to the learning?	
❑ How will I include meaningful student engagements in the allotted time?	
❑ How will I pace the lesson to keep all students active and participating?	
❑ What routines will I utilize to exclude nonproductive time?	
❑ How will I share this information with my students?	
❑ How will I check that my students understand the goals of effective pacing?	
❑ How will my students understand that reflecting on the instructional aspects of the learning supports ownership of their learning?	

Table 2.8: Questions to Guide Implementing Strategic Learning Practice, Instruction 3

Implementing the Practice

How did Mr. Lee use the questions in table 2.8 to help plan how he would offer support to his students? First, he had to determine the following:

▸ What skill will my students learn, and how will they demonstrate they have learned it?

Mr. Lee says, "We are focusing on the following standard: 'Given a geometric figure and a rotation, reflection, or translation, draw the transformed figure using, e.g., graph paper, tracing paper, or geometry software. Specify a sequence of transformations that will carry a given figure onto another.' We have learned about each transformation separately. Today I need to make certain the students understand them all and can differentiate one from the other. It's easy for students to confuse them. I knew I wanted them to have varied practice with the skill, so we will use both trace paper and the geometry software program. I also knew I would need them to articulate their learning because justifications are a must.

"This could be a lot for one class period, so I knew we would have to start right away and have quick transitions."

Mr. Lee then had to answer the following questions:

▸ How much time will I allot to the learning?

▸ How will I include meaningful student engagements in the allotted time?

▸ How will I pace the lesson to keep all students active and participating?

▸ What routines will I utilize to exclude nonproductive time?

Mr. Lee continues, "Since we have learned about each transformation, I was confident we could apply the learning in a variety of ways. I wanted to make sure the students had more than one opportunity to cement their understanding for each of them. And we only have this class period for this learning. I needed to utilize all of my routines to make sure we didn't waste any time.

"For example, we begin each class with a warm-up activity. The students know that it begins once they enter the room. They know to look up, read the activity expectation, and get to work. I used to tell them how much time they had. Now I have a timer on the screen that really helps them stay on task. When the timer goes off, we get back together and go over the objective for the day. I never vary this routine. Each day begins the same way. This has also kept me on track.

"Next, we always review the objective. After that, I introduce the learning plan for the day. Today they will first complete the tracing-paper activity. Once completed, they have to check in with me for accuracy and be prepared to justify their answers. Once they complete this accurately, they move onto the iPad activity.

"We have a routine for iPad use. I know some teachers tend not to use them as they find there is too much hassle in keeping them charged and organized. We have an iPad cart and a set procedure for checking them out and returning them. I put that task onto the students. We decided on a process at the beginning of the year. They understand that they have to own their role in the process in order to utilize the iPads, which they love to use.

"We also have set routines when it comes to peer conversations—we don't have time to have them talk about anything other than geometry. And I need them to practice talking to all types of thinkers. I initially assigned them their partners, but once they showed me they were ready, I let them select their own. We do this each week."

But Mr. Lee wanted to help his students own this information so that he could increase the probability of their learning. To do this, he had to determine the following:

- How will I share this information with my students?
- How will I check that my students understand the goals of effective pacing?

Mr. Lee explains, "At the beginning of the year, I share the math standards for the course with each class. We discuss what the expectations of learning are for the year. I assure my students that my job is to make certain each student is successful, but this can only occur if we work as a class and really respect our math time. For the first couple of weeks, I introduce the routines we will use. I don't just tell them what the routine is, but why it is important to help us be superefficient and ensure that we, as a class, meet all of the course learning expectations. I know teenagers—I know I will have to continually review the routines throughout the year if we want to stay on course.

What I love is that the students began to monitor each other. You will hear one student tell another to get back to work. We don't have time to waste!"

Mr. Lee was very interested in making sure his students understood the value of owning their own learning. Thus, he had to ask himself the following question:

▸ How will my students understand that reflecting on the instructional aspects of the learning supports ownership of their learning?

Mr. Lee goes on by saying, "Our classes are bookended. We begin each class with a warm-up, and we end with a reflection. We share what we learned and how the lesson went. I ask my students to reflect on the pace of the lesson. Were parts of it too fast? Why or why not? Were parts too slow? I need them to see that I am always striving to make our learning more efficient. We also talk about their role in this—what went well and what needs to be improved. My favorite days are when they look up and realize the class is almost over and say, 'Wow, today went fast.' When that happens, I know I planned a good lesson."

Teachers like Mr. Lee have realized that without this support—ensuring all time is devoted to the learning, implementing routines that support the efficient use of instructional time, and offering sufficient and appropriate time for the determined objective—his students will struggle with owning their learning.

What Teachers Are Doing

What are other ways teachers have implemented this practice—"Each and every student is supported by **opportunities** for **meaningful engagement** in which **instructional time** is used **efficiently**"—as they offer support for developing student ownership?

Take this example from a biology teacher: "Because the content is so dense in high school science, it is important that my students know exactly what is going to happen in class on a daily basis. That is why they read the learning objective as soon as they walk in the door. We then discuss anything that needs to be clarified. At the beginning of the year, this routine took some time—I wrote it on the board, they discussed it with each other, and I clarified any questions they had. After a while, I wrote the objective at the top of the day's agenda that they found in their Chromebooks. They still discussed it but without my guidance. A few minutes were saved this way. By spring, the students knew that they needed to understand the day's objective before we could begin. Some even came to class having read the agenda before the bell rang. The time needed to get the class going became shorter and shorter throughout the year. The kids knew the routine and followed it."

Take this example from an elementary teacher: "For my certification process, I had to record and reflect on one of my lessons. I quickly realized that I had too much downtime during transitions, both within a lesson and between lessons. I went to some of my colleagues and asked them what routines they had in place for transitions. The best piece of advice I got was to choose one routine and teach it well. I would have to define it for myself at the highest level. I would also have to model it, have clear expectations, model it again, reflect on it, and so on. Once I had it in place, I would add another. I now have a bank of routines that I use in my class. It has saved so much time."

Take this example from a middle school industrial arts teacher: "I made student conversations a priority this year. But I found it was taking too much time, and some students finished talking earlier and others seemed to need more time. I realized I had two problems. First, I needed better questions that gave the students more to discuss. But I also realized I didn't need every student to get to the 'end' of their conversation. My real goal was to have them express their thinking and push their learning at that moment. Once I had that goal clear, pacing became easier. I began to give my students a little less time than I thought they needed, and I used a timer. I needed them to have a sense of urgency and get their thinking out. I didn't need every student to talk until they ran out of things to say."

What Students Are Saying

What do students say about this practice—"Each and every student is supported by **opportunities** for **meaningful engagement** in which **instructional time** is used **efficiently**"—and its support for the ownership of their learning?

Take this example from a high school student: "My trigonometry teacher runs a tight ship. We walk in the class and start right away. But I don't mind it. We learn so much, and the class goes by so quickly. Other classes seem to take forever, and sometimes I don't even know the point. Mr. Garcia makes sure we know what the objective is every day, and then every minute we work on it. Some days my brain hurts when I leave his class."

Take this example from a kindergarten student: "We get to do centers every day. Our chart tells us where to go. We have to put our center back neatly before it ends. When Mrs. Lacey puts on the song, we have to clean up and come to the rug before the song ends."

Take this example from a seventh grader: "The routines we use in our science class have helped me organize better. The way we organize our notebooks and the way we take notes help me because I can do it the same way in other classes. My mom tells me that my backpack now doesn't look like a black hole. I also am more comfortable talking to other kids—in science we have to justify our answers, and the teacher makes us talk to everyone. I know how to begin a conversation and share my ideas. Even in classes that aren't as organized, I can still begin a conversation and share my ideas fairly quickly."

Instruction Reflection

How Well Do You Develop Students to Own How They Are Learning?

In this chapter, we have shown you what student ownership looks like in practice. We have shown you what it sounds like when students own their part in instruction. And we have given examples of how teachers have implemented these strategic learning practices in a variety of classrooms.

We have also explained the difference between a student who is simply *doing* or *understanding* instruction and one who is *owning* what they are learning.

A student is *doing* when they can state how they need to complete the task in front on them.

A student is *understanding* when they can explain what strategy they are engaged in.

A student is *owning* how they are learning when they can articulate the strategy they are currently using to learn, how this strategy supports their learning, and how they will use this strategy in the future—during the class, in other classes, and when they are working on their own.

Think of your students. Where do they fall on the doing-understanding-owning continuum? Think about the supports they need from you to develop student ownership. How often and to what degree do you offer these supports? In other words, what impact do you have on student ownership?

Remember what John Hattie (2011) said: "Such passion for evaluating impact is the single most critical lever for instructional excellence—accompanied by understanding this impact, and doing something in light of the evidence and understanding" (pg. viii).

What follows are reflection activities that will help you determine your impact on student ownership—both areas of strength and areas of growth.

In order to develop student ownership, all student learning must be driven by highly engaging, effective, and efficient instruction.

And, as always, your actions are key to the development of student ownership.

Reflect on Strategic Learning Practice, Instruction 1

Each and every student is supported by opportunities for meaningful engagement using structured student-to-student communication.

Consider how your students respond to the following questions:

▸ How does engaging in conversations with my peers push my learning?

▸ How do I participate in these conversations?

▸ What is my role as both a speaker and a listener?

Think about your students' responses—remembering that your support is directly linked to developing student ownership—and use the following to help you reflect on the strengths and gaps of your support.

How often and how well do you offer these supports?

- Student communications build toward mastery of the relevant standards and measurable and achievable learning outcomes.

_____

- Multiple and varied opportunities for student communication are provided.

_____

- Student communications are structured to provide rigorous and high-quality conversations.

_____

- Structured communications include reciprocal speaking and listening opportunities for each student.

Table 2.9: Reflect on Strategic Learning Practice, Instruction 1

Reflect on Strategic Learning Practice, Instruction 2

Each and every student is supported by opportunities for meaningful engagement using effective instructional strategies.

Consider how your students respond to the following questions:

▸ How does engaging in this instructional strategy support my learning?

▸ How can I use this instructional strategy in the future?

▸ What is the value of reflecting on my learning?

Think about your students' responses—remembering that your support is directly linked to developing student ownership—and use the following to help you reflect on the strengths and gaps of your support.

How often and how well do you offer these supports?

• Instructional strategies build toward mastery of the relevant standards and measurable and achievable learning outcomes.

_____

• Instructional strategies require a high level of active participation.

_____

• Instructional strategies account for the differing needs of your students.

_____

• Reflection on the purpose and value of the instructional strategy is required of students.

Table 2.10: Reflect on Strategic Learning Practice, Instruction 2

Reflect on Strategic Learning Practice, Instruction 3

Each and every student is supported by opportunities for meaningful engagement in which instructional time is used efficiently.

Consider how your students respond to the following questions:

▸ How much time do I have to learn this?

▸ How can I use my time most efficiently?

▸ How can these routines help me in the future?

Think about your students' responses—remembering that your support is directly linked to developing student ownership—and use the following to help you reflect on the strengths and gaps of your support.

How often and how well do you offer these supports?

- All time is used to meaningfully engage students toward mastery of the relevant standards and measurable and achievable learning outcomes.

_____

- The pace keeps all students actively participating.

_____

- Routines are used to maximize instructional time and exclude nonproductive time.

Table 2.11: Reflect on Strategic Learning Practice, Instruction 3

3 ASSESSMENT

Developing Students to Own How Well They Are Learning

For many teachers, assessment occurs at the end of the lesson, unit, or course. It is used primarily to determine what the student knows or doesn't know. Almost all assessments are viewed as summative, and the vast majority are some kind of formalized test. Teachers then discuss students in terms of their test scores—Jose received 98 percent on the midterm and is ready for geometry; Erika got an F on the midterm and needs to repeat algebra 1. Thus, in most classrooms, we find assessment *of* learning, not assessment *for* learning. This is why we hear students say that the teacher "gave me that grade" and not "I made the decision to earn that grade."

This approach to assessment tends to make the teacher the focus—they are the final judge of what students know or don't know. We need to flip this to make the student the focus—*they* are the judge of their own knowledge and skills. True student ownership begins when the teacher looks at assessment from the point of view of the student. That is assessment for learning.

Assessment is defined as the student's ability to understand when they are learning and when they are struggling. This understanding directly relates to the learning as determined in curriculum and to the strategies as determined in instruction. In other words, once a student knows what they are learning, how they will learn it, and how they will show they have learned it, they can then identify—every step of the way—if they are learning and if they are struggling. They will better understand the data that tells them whether they are learning or struggling. This means students know the value of consistent checking for understanding. It also means that students know when they need to ask for help.

The Imperatives for Ownership of Assessment

To develop student ownership, several things are imperative: It is imperative for students to know and be able to articulate when they are learning and when they are struggling. It is imperative for students to identify those strategies that help them when they are learning. It is imperative for students to identify when they are struggling and to find the supports they need to continue learning. It is imperative for students to accept feedback as a means for learning and to offer feedback to others. It is imperative that students identify their own strengths and areas of need. It is imperative for students to know how their strengths support their learning. It is imperative for students to know that their areas of need can be supported and that these supports can be used in a variety of settings.

Table 3.1 provides some helpful indicators that reveal when students are taking ownership of their learning.

How Do Students Demonstrate Ownership of Assessment?

Each and every student is able to articulate:

- what they are learning and how they will demonstrate they have learned it,
- how they are learning,
- how well they are learning,
- when they are learning and how they know they are learning,
- when they are struggling and how they know they are struggling,
- how checking for understanding and feedback, both affirmative and corrective, supports them in their learning,
- what supports they might need from the teacher when learning is not occurring,
- what strategies they might use to continue learning,
- their individual areas of need,
- what supports they require to address their individual areas of need, and
- why understanding these aspects of assessment helps them own their learning.

Table 3.1: Indicators of Student Ownership of Assessment

Graham Nuthall (2007) clarifies the value of student-centered assessment: "But whatever you intend, in order to know if you have been effective, you must have some way of knowing what your students believed, know, could do, or felt before you taught them and what your students believed, knew, could do, or felt after you taught them. Learning, of whatever kind, is about change, and unless you know what has changed in the minds, skills, and attitudes of your students, you cannot really know how effective you have been" (p. 35).

However, teachers cannot know what has changed in the minds, skills, or attitudes of their students unless the students are part of the process—unless students own their role in identifying when they are learning and when they are struggling. As explained in chapter 2, the value of student-centered assessment is found in the research around metacognition and the regulation of cognition. Students who regulate their own learning are developing ownership of their learning.

Putting Student Ownership into Practice

But what does student ownership look like in practice? What does it sound like when a student owns their part in assessment? What is the difference between a student who is simply *doing* or *understanding* assessment and one who is *owning* how well they are learning?

A student is *doing* when they can state how they will finish the task in front of them.

A student is *understanding* when they can explain how they know they are learning.

A student is *owning* how well they are learning when they can articulate if they are learning or struggling and why, what to do if they are learning or struggling, and how assessing their learning helps them learn more.

The tables that follow—table 3.2, table 3.3, table 3.4, and table 3.5—present some examples of what this looks and sounds like on a continuum of doing-understanding-owing in a variety of content areas and grade levels, particularly when we ask the question, "How well are you learning?"

Possible responses on the continuum from kindergarten students in social studies when asked,

"How well are you learning?"

"My picture shows me taking turns. I can read my picture and my friends' pictures to know all of the rules. If I don't know a rule, they will tell me. I know that when I can say all the rules, then I have learned the rules. I have a few more to learn."

"This is a picture of me sharing. I shared blocks with my friend. I know this is a rule."

"I drew a good picture."

DOING   UNDERSTANDING   OWNING

Table 3.2: Student Ownership Continuum, Social Studies, Grade K

Possible responses on the continuum from fifth grade students in math when asked,

"How well are you learning?"

"Today we are learning to subtract decimals. Once we finish a problem we ask our partner, "How did you get that?" and, "How do you know if you subtracted correctly?" We will use addition to show how we have subtracted correctly. If it is wrong, we will work together to find out where we made a mistake and fix it. We don't have to wait for the teacher to tell us."

"We are subtracting decimals. Once I solve the problem, I use addition to see if it is correct. This helps me know if my math is getting better."

"We have a quiz on Friday that will tell me."

DOING   UNDERSTANDING   OWNING

Table 3.3: Student Ownership Continuum, Math, Grade 5

Possible responses on the continuum from seventh grade students in English-language arts when asked,

"How well are you learning?"

"We have a rubric that tells us the components of an effective argument, including an introduction with a claim that is supported with evidence. My partner read my first draft and gave me feedback. Now I am highlighting where I introduced my claim and supported it. My writing is much better when I know beforehand the components of a strong essay because I can check to see if I have included each piece or not."

"We are writing argument essays. The teacher shared the rubric that will be used when he scores our final essays. I use it to check my writing."

"The teacher grades our essays and tells us."

DOING   UNDERSTANDING   OWNING

Table 3.4: Student Ownership Continuum, English-Language Arts, Grade 7

Possible responses on the continuum from tenth grade students in science when asked,

"How well are you learning?"

"We are learning about changes in the composition of the nucleus of the atom and the energy released during the processes of fission and fusion. It can get confusing at times, so we are developing models that demonstrate this. I have discovered if I can't see something, then I have a hard time remembering it. My teacher says I am a visual learner. With each model, I refer back to my notes to make sure my information is accurate."

"I will turn in my model that shows the changes in the composition of the nucleus of the atom. I think I did a good job."

"I will fill out the exit ticket."

DOING   UNDERSTANDING   OWNING

Table 3.5: Student Ownership Continuum, Science, Grade 10

Moving to Student Ownership

What can a teacher do to move a student toward owning their learning? Student ownership is best defined as a mindset. Students who know they have the authority, capacity, and responsibility to own their learning possess an ownership mindset. Thus, to move a student, the teacher must delegate the authority, build the capacity, and give the responsibility to each and every student.

How does a teacher do this? They must model the thinking behind the ownership and explicitly teach the skills of ownership. This takes planning. In order for students to answer the questions posed earlier—"How will I know I have learned it?", "How will I know I am progressing in my learning?", and "What can I do if I am struggling?"—teachers must be strategic in the practices they use to increase learning.

While there are hundreds of actions a teacher must take in a day, we will focus on those three practices in assessment that research shows increase the opportunities for learning—by increasing the opportunities for student ownership.

Teachers must strategically decide when to offer the following three learning practices:

- **Strategic Learning Practice, Assessment 1:** Each and every student is supported by data that is used to monitor current understanding and provide feedback.

- **Strategic Learning Practice, Assessment 2:** Each and every student is supported by data that is used to monitor current understanding and adjust as needed.

- **Strategic Learning Practice, Assessment 3:** Each and every student is supported by data that is used to differentiate based on predetermined student needs.

In the following sections, we will clearly define each learning practice, describe what implementation looks and sounds like in the classroom, share teacher planning questions, offer examples of how students have been supported with these learning practices in a variety of content areas and grade levels, and explain how these practices directly lead to increased student ownership.

Strategic Learning Practice, Assessment 1

Each and Every Student Is Supported by Data That Is Used to Monitor Current Understanding and Provide Feedback

In order for students to own their learning in regard to assessment, each and every student must be able to answer the following questions:

▸ Are you learning, and how do you know?

▸ Are you struggling, and how do you know?

▸ How does checking for understanding and receiving feedback support your learning?

In order for teachers to develop students who own their learning in regard to assessment, it is imperative that teachers support students with practices that are strategically implemented on a daily basis. The teacher needs to focus on those practices that Hattie and Temperley (2007), Kulhavy (1997), Kluger and DeNisi (1996), Samson, Strykowski, Weinstein, and Walberg (1987), and Fendick (1990) show increase the opportunities for learning by increasing the opportunities for student ownership. Strategic Learning Practice, Assessment 1, states: "Each and every student is supported by **data** that is used to **monitor current understanding** and **provide feedback**."

First, let's define each aspect of this practice.

Data is any information that is gathered to indicate whether the students are learning the designated outcomes for the unit or lesson. This data can be an informal conversation with an individual student, a whole-class check for understanding, or a more formal quiz or test.

Monitor assumes the teacher is consistently checking to see if students are learning or struggling.

Current understanding refers to the intended learning at that specific moment in the unit or lesson.

Provide feedback refers to information from the teacher that is communicated to the students to affirm, clarify, or redirect their learning.

The Practice in Action

What does this practice—"Each and every student is supported by **data** that is used to **monitor current understanding** and **provide feedback**"—look like in a classroom at the highest level? You might walk into Mrs. Thompson's sixth-grade math class and read the following learning outcome on the board: "Students will relate decimals to mixed numbers to find and explain the sums and differences of decimals."

That is what the students read. But what happens when you ask them questions about their learning?

You: "What are you learning?"

Student: "I am learning how to solve addition and subtraction problems that have mixed numbers in them. We are learning how to convert them into decimals. This makes them easier to solve."

You: "How well are you doing with this learning?"

Student: "I'm doing pretty good. I am able to solve most of the problems."

You: "Does solving them tell you that you have learned?"

Student: "Well, kind of. That is just one part of it. For each problem, there are several steps we have to follow. You can see I have them here in my notebook. In the first step, we have to read the problem. Mrs. Thompson makes us read it out loud to ourselves in a soft voice to make sure we are saying—I mean expressing—the numbers correctly. In the second step, we have to convert the mixed numbers into decimals. In the third step, we have to round the addends to the nearest whole number and find the estimated answer—I mean sum. In the fourth step, we add the decimals, making sure we line them up correctly. In the fifth step, we compare our answer to the estimated sum. In the sixth step, we explain our process and math to our partner. We get feedback on how we did."

You: "What does feedback sound like?"

Student: "The feedback has to be about the math we just explained. If I explain it well, Mrs. Thompson will tell me specifically what I did right. She doesn't just say, 'Good job' or, 'You got it right.' She tells me why I did a good job or why my answer was right. Also, if I got something wrong, she will give me feedback on that. She doesn't just tell me I was wrong or just give me the answer. She tells me something that will help me figure it out. In one of the problems, I did not line up the decimals correctly. She told me to look back at that step and asked me to remember what we learned about aligning decimals. That helped me. We are now learning how to give feedback to one another. If my partner explained something but it didn't make sense to me, I might ask them a question so they could explain it again."

You: "How does receiving feedback tell you how well you are learning?"

Student: "Each time I follow the process and get feedback, I go faster and I get more problems right. I also don't have to use my notes very much. We want to be able to solve these problems without our notes. We have to learn the process. If I can follow the process without looking at my notes, then I know I'm doing well. But mostly I know I'm doing well when I can explain it in my own words. Mrs. Thompson tells us that the more we talk about our learning, the more we will understand and own our learning. Right now I can explain it well to my partner."

You: "What happens if you are struggling with the learning?"

Student: "First, I go back to my notes, look at the process, and see where I may have made a mistake. Then I can talk with my partner. If I still need help, I go to Mrs. Thompson."

Are you wondering how the student was able to answer your questions so clearly and with such confidence? Let's ask Mrs. Thompson.

"I am a firm believer in ongoing assessment and strong feedback. I need my students to understand that learning is a process. I don't expect them to master something right away. I also cannot have my students wait until quizzes and tests to find out how they are doing. And *I* can't wait until then either. I have too many students to wait until after I've graded papers to find out if learning is occurring. I need to know all along the way, and I need *them* to know along the way. With modeling, my students have taken on the role of assessing their learning and supporting one another. This has saved me so much time and energy."

Mrs. Thompson used the Strategic Learning Practice, Assessment 1, as a frame to help her plan how she wanted to offer this support. This frame is flexible and fits the needs of both teachers and students. However, the following planning questions in table 3.6 helped her focus the support.

Questions to Guide Implementing Strategic Learning Practice, Assessment 1:

Each and every student is supported by data that is used to monitor current understanding and provide feedback.

Use these planning questions to focus your support.

	Notes
❏ What skill will my students learn, and how will they demonstrate they have learned it?	
❏ How and when will I monitor understanding throughout the lesson?	
❏ How will these data checks tie directly to the learning outcome?	
❏ How will feedback be delivered to clarify understanding?	
❏ How will feedback be delivered to build toward mastery of the learning outcome?	
❏ How will I share this information with my students?	
❏ How will I check that my students understand their progress toward the goals of the unit or lesson?	
❏ How will my students understand that reflecting on their learning supports ownership of their learning?	

Table 3.6: Questions to Guide Implementing Strategic Learning Practice, Assessment 1

Implementing the Practice

How did Mrs. Thompson use the questions in table 3.6 to help plan how she would offer support to her students? First, she had to determine the following:

▸ What skill will my students learn, and how will they demonstrate they have learned it?

Mrs. Thompson explains, "We are learning standard 6.NS.3: 'Fluently add, subtract, multiply, and divide multi-digit decimals using the standard algorithm for each operation.' Right now we are focusing on the addition and subtraction of mixed numbers. I knew I needed my students to bring together lots of understandings in this lesson. I needed to reinforce number sense of fractions and decimals with careful attention to how we express numbers. I needed to reinforce approximations by having them round and get estimated sums. I needed to reinforce the relationship between fractions and decimals. And I needed to reinforce the computation of the addition and subtraction of decimals. There is a lot that my students need to practice in this lesson, and I have to check for understanding for all of it."

Mrs. Thompson then had to determine the answers to the following questions:

▸ How and when will I monitor understanding throughout the lesson?

▸ How will these data checks tie directly to the learning outcome?

Mrs. Thompson says, "I knew I had a lot to monitor for, and that I had to plan specifically how, when, and what I was going to check for. In this lesson, the students are applying the learning, both independently and with a partner. This gives me the flexibility to move about the room and observe, listen, and speak with students about the learning. I have created a chart I keep on a clipboard to monitor each student's progress. It includes what learning targets I am looking for and each student's name. As I move about the room, I am careful to mark what learning targets I am seeing and hearing, and which ones I am not. The student names keep me on task for checking in with all learners."

Mrs. Thompson then had to determine the following:

▸ How will feedback be delivered to clarify understanding?

▸ How will feedback be delivered to build toward mastery of the learning outcome?

Mrs. Thompson continues, "As I stated earlier, I know the importance of strong feedback to learning. I also realized along the way that I can't be the only one giving feedback in my class. I needed the support of the students. Throughout the year, I have modeled why and how we give feedback. In this lesson, this is the first time feedback is a required step. Student partners must share their thinking and their process, and they must support each other with specific feedback to affirm, clarify, or redirect the learning. As I monitor, I am doing two things. I am listening to the level of feedback they are giving one another to see where they may need more support with this. I am also talking with students about their learning and providing them with feedback."

But Mrs. Thompson wanted to ensure that her students would be able to use the skills in a variety of situations. She wanted to help her students own this information so that she could increase the probability of their learning. To do that, she then had to ask herself the following questions:

▸ How will I share this information with my students?

▸ How will I check that my students understand their progress toward the goals of the unit or lesson?

Mrs. Thompson says, "I let my students know that learning is a process. At the beginning of the year, we review the math standards for the entire year. We understand that we have until the end of the school year to master these standards. I let them know along the way where we are. Am I just initially introducing a new skill to them? Are we practicing a new skill? Are they independently applying a new skill? Are they transferring a skill into a new situation or concept? I have had students come to me thinking they are already unsuccessful in math and the year hasn't even started. The clearer they are in the course goals, the unit goals, and the lesson goals, the clearer they are in where we are in the process and the more they can relax and learn. But I need them to be a part of assessment process along the way. I need them to understand their role in supporting one another's learning and providing strong feedback. Students understand this after some work. I used to feel like I was the only one supporting 120 sixth graders. There are now 121 of us assessing and supporting along the way."

Mrs. Thompson is committed to ensuring that her sixth graders understand the value of owning their own learning. Thus, she has to determine the following:

▶ How will my students understand that reflecting on their learning supports ownership of their learning?

Mrs. Thompson continues by saying, "We end every lesson and every unit with a reflection of our learning. Students report where they feel they are in the process. My students can now tell me when they need more support, when they need different models, when they need more practice, and so on. We also discuss feedback. I have them report on what specific feedback they received that affirmed, clarified, or redirected their learning and how. I have them report on what specific feedback they gave that affirmed, clarified, or redirected someone else's learning. They see the value in this."

Teachers like Mrs. Thompson have realized that without this support—multiple opportunities for students to let the teacher know if they are learning or struggling; receiving feedback that affirms, clarifies, or redirects their learning; and understanding the value of articulating their progress—her students will struggle with owning their learning.

What Teachers Are Doing

What are other ways teachers have implemented this practice—"Each and every student is supported by **data** that is used to **monitor current understanding** and **provide feedback**"—as they offer support for developing student ownership?

Take this example from a seventh-grade language arts teacher: "I've realized that the most efficient way for me to check for understanding of my whole class is to have my students talk to one another—a lot. Not only does listening in let me see where they are in terms of content, but it also lets me check on other skills. For my English learners, I can listen to their current grasp of the language and either offer feedback right then or use the information for support later on."

Take this example from a high school algebra 2 class: "I tell my classes that I need to give clear and specific feedback if it is to be effective. But there are times when I forget. So, whenever I just say, 'Nice job' or, 'Great work,' I have told my students to stop me and ask, 'Can you tell me why, please?' They understand that specific feedback—positive or corrective—is more supportive for their learning."

Take this example from a third-grade teacher: "I know that my colleagues tell me that they never know how often to check for understanding. I tell them that I check at every transition in the lesson. If my students must know something before they can attend to the next part, that's a time for me to check for understanding."

Take this example from a middle school principal: "I see my teachers using a lot of different strategies to check for understanding. Some ask questions and have students share with one another. Some use whiteboards and have students show their work. Some use thumbs-up or thumbs-down to get the read of an entire classroom. Some use a ticket-out-the-door that gives them information about the lesson. I am less concerned about the method of gathering information than I am about what the teacher or students do with it."

Take this example from a fourth-grade teacher: "I recently went to a workshop and was told that giving students feedback was one of the top methods to increase learning. The presenter also said that receiving feedback was one of the top supports that students requested. It just reminded me how much we all want to know how we are doing and, if we're struggling, what we can do differently. This changed my feelings about feedback, and my students are telling me how important it is for them. In fact, I am teaching my kids to offer feedback to one another."

What Students Are Saying

What do students say about this practice—"Each and every student is supported by **data** that is used to **monitor current understanding** and **provide feedback**"—and its support for the ownership of their learning?

Take this example for a first grader: "Miss January is always telling us what we are doing right and when we need help. Today, I was writing a sentence, and she told me that I had started each sentence with a capital letter and ended each with a period. This will remind me to do it the same way next time."

Take this example from a middle school student: "I really like getting feedback. Sometimes I just don't know if I am getting it or not, and it helps me to be told what is going on. Sometimes, when I hear what the teacher is telling me, I think, 'I should have known that!' But the more feedback I get, the more I am reminded that I do know stuff and that I just need to put it all together."

Strategic Learning Practice, Assessment 2

Each and Every Student Is Supported by Data That Is Used to Monitor Current Understanding and Adjust as Needed

In order for students to own their learning in regard to assessment, each and every student must be able to answer the following questions:

- ▶ Are you struggling, and how do you know?

- ▶ What supports might you need from the teacher?

- ▶ What strategies might you use to continue learning?

In order for teachers to develop students who own their learning in regard to assessment, it is imperative that teachers support students with practices that are strategically implemented on a daily basis. This requires a focus on those practices that Fuchs and Fuchs (1986) show increase the opportunities for learning by increasing the opportunities for student ownership. Strategic Learning Practice, Assessment 2, states: "Each and every student is supported by **data** that is used to **monitor current understanding** and **adjust as needed**."

First, let's define each aspect of this practice.

Data is any information that is gathered to indicate if the students are learning the designated outcomes for a unit or lesson. This data can be an informal conversation with an individual student, a whole-class check for understanding, or a more formal quiz or test.

Monitor assumes the teacher is consistently checking to see if students are learning or struggling.

Current understanding refers to the intended learning at that specific moment in the unit or lesson.

Adjust implies modifying the instruction to provide more support for those who are struggling or to accelerate the pace for those who are succeeding more quickly than anticipated.

As needed implies that the teacher utilizes the information from the monitoring to determine whether to adjust.

The Practice in Action

What does this practice—"Each and every student is supported by **data** that is used to **monitor current understanding** and **adjust as needed**"— look like in a classroom at the highest level? You might visit Mrs. Cruz's high school biology class. As you walk in, you notice the goal of the unit on the board: "Construct an explanation based on evidence for how the structure of DNA determines the structure of proteins, which carry out the essential functions of life through systems of specialized cells." You then notice today's goal: "Analyze how the sequence of genes contains instructions that code for proteins in order to gather evidence for your DNA explanation."

That is what your see on the board. But what happens when you talk to students and ask them about their learning?

You: "What are you learning?"

Student: "We are analyzing how the sequence of genes contains instructions that code for proteins. That's what it says on the board."

You: "What does that mean?"

Student: "I'm not 100 percent sure just yet. But Mrs. Cruz is going to have us discuss with one another what we think it means, and then she will point out what we already know and will help us clarify what we don't understand."

You: "Does she do that often?"

Student: "Yes. She tells us that we need to know if we are getting it or if we are struggling. If we are struggling, she says she wants us to figure out why so that she can help us better."

You: "Are you struggling? How do you know?"

Student: "Actually, I am. Right now I am stuck on how the genes are sequenced. I just can't see it. When I talk to my friends, they are having the same issue."

You: "What supports might you need from the teacher?"

Student: "Well, we told her we were struggling with understanding the sequence, and she asked the class who else was struggling. Most of the class raised their hands. She then asked us to talk with our partners and come up with a couple of ways she could help us. Some kids wanted her to explain it again. Some kids wanted more time to talk with one another. But most of us told her we needed to see it. She then drew a DNA strand on the whiteboard using a lot of different colors to represent different genes. She had us talk to one another and define the different colors. Then she asked us to draw the DNA model in our science notebooks. She erased the board and asked us to close our notebooks and tell our partners what we remembered. This worked well."

You: "What strategies might you use to continue learning?"

Student: "I like the idea of drawing information. The drawing really helps me see it. I think I will try to draw information whenever I am stuck. Mrs. Cruz said that this was called visual learning, so I must be a visual learner. She also said that she was surprised how many students needed the visuals. She said she would try to incorporate as many visuals as possible to help us learn. I like Mrs. Cruz's class because she will change things if we are stuck."

Are you wondering how the student was able to explain how well they were learning, or not, with such confidence and clarity? Let's ask Mrs. Cruz how she set up her class.

"Science is scary for many of my students. It is very important that my students know when they are learning and when they are struggling. But most importantly, I need them to identify what is working or not working for them. I understand these science concepts so well that I sometimes forget about the struggle. But I need them to help me out and to tell me what they need in order to understand the concepts. Sometimes it is a completely different approach than the one I had planned."

Mrs. Cruz used the Strategic Learning Practice, Assessment 2, as a frame to help her plan how she wanted to offer this support. This frame is flexible and fits the needs of both teachers and students. However, the following planning questions in table 3.7 helped her focus the support.

Questions to Guide Implementing Strategic Learning Practice, Assessment 2:

Each and every student is supported by data that is used to monitor current understanding and adjust as needed.

Use these planning questions to focus your support.

	Notes
❑ What skill will my students learn, and how will they demonstrate they have learned it?	
❑ How and when will I check for understanding throughout the lesson?	
❑ How will these data checks tie directly to the learning outcome?	
❑ How could I adjust the instruction if students are struggling?	
❑ How could I adjust the instruction if students are succeeding more quickly than anticipated?	
❑ How will I share this information with my students?	
❑ How will I check that my students understand their progress toward the goals of the unit or lesson?	
❑ How will my students understand that reflecting on their learning supports ownership of their learning?	

Table 3.7: Questions to Guide Implementing Strategic Learning Practice, Assessment 2

Implementing the Practice

How did the questions in table 3.7 help Mrs. Cruz plan how she would offer support to her students? First, she had to determine the following:

▸ What skill will my students learn, and how will they demonstrate they have learned it?

Mrs. Cruz says, "We are at the beginning of our unit on DNA and cells, so I selected the following performance expectation: 'Construct an explanation based on evidence for how the structure of DNA determines the structure of proteins which carry out the essential functions of life through systems of specialized cells.' This expectation told me exactly what the students needed to do—construct an explanation based on evidence. Today, I will tell the class the sequence of cells in DNA. Fairly easy concept to begin with, so I will use a straight lecture format with various checks for understanding throughout."

Mrs. Cruz then had to ask the following questions:

▸ How and when will I check for understanding throughout the lesson?

▸ How will these data checks tie directly to the learning outcome?

Mrs. Cruz explains, "First, I will have students read and review the learning outcome. They will discuss with one another and identify what they already know and what will be new learning. I will listen in and clarify misunderstandings. Throughout the lecture, I will stop and have the students review the learning outcome and determine where they are in the process of learning. Again, I will listen in and clarify misunderstandings."

Next, Mrs. Cruz needed to think about the following question:

▸ How could I adjust the instruction if students are struggling?

Mrs. Cruz continues, "While planning the lesson, I think about the various strategies I could use to teach my students. I choose the one that makes the most sense for the learning outcome and that class. However, I do understand that not every strategy works for every student. So, if I see that a majority of my class is struggling, I will ask them to tell me what they need. Sometimes they want me to explain it again. Sometimes they want to spend more time talking with one another. Sometimes they need to see the information in a different way. Sometimes I need to go in a different direction.

"That's what happened today. It became apparent that the concept of DNA and how the genes are sequenced was much more difficult for my students than I had previously thought. When I asked them what they needed to understand it, many said that they needed to see it. This seems so obvious that I'm embarrassed to say I had not even thought about it that way. When I drew the color visual on the whiteboard and saw their faces, it reminded me just how many visual leaners I had in my classroom. They let me know this really worked for them. This adjustment was just what they needed and is something I will incorporate in future lessons."

Mrs. Cruz also had to plan for the opposite by answering the following question:

▸ How could I adjust the instruction if students are succeeding more quickly than anticipated?

Mrs. Cruz says, "This is much easier. Because I understand my course expectations and how each unit is structured, I can backward map all of my lessons. So, if students are understanding faster than I thought, I just move into the new lesson. Because my students know the expectations of the unit, they don't struggle if a lesson doesn't fit into a perfect forty-eight-minute period."

Because Mrs. Cruz believes that deeper learning occurs when students have to struggle, she wants her students to be comfortable with determining when they are learning and why and when they are struggling and why. She also wants them to have a variety of strategies to use to help them continue learning.

Mrs. Cruz had to determine the following:

▸ How will I share this information with my students?

▸ How will I check that my students understand their progress toward the goals of the unit or lesson?

Mrs. Cruz explains, "I tell my students that I am a guide to help them learn more. I cannot pour the knowledge into their brains—they must play an active role in their own learning. This means they must know if they are learning or if they are struggling. They can't sit there passively waiting for a test or the teacher to tell them. Once they have determined their progress toward mastery, I ask them to think about reasons why this might be happening. It's as equally important to identify what is working for them when they are learning as it is to identify what is not working for them when they are struggling. This type of thinking ties nicely with the science and engineering practices, and it models for my students how scientists think about and reflect on their work. I want them to consider science as an option for college or their career."

This thinking shows that Mrs. Cruz wants her students to own their learning. She needs to think about the following question:

▸ How will my students understand that reflecting on their learning supports ownership of their learning?

Mrs. Cruz says, "We spent a lot of time discussing how scientists think and do their jobs. Because scientists are always trying to answer a new question or are trying to find a solution to a new problem, they must clearly determine what they know already and what they will have to learn. Scientists own what they know, what they need to learn, and how they need to learn it. I tell my students that my job is to have them think like a scientist."

Teachers like Mrs. Cruz have realized that without this support—multiple opportunities for students to let the teacher know if they are learning or struggling, different instruction and pacing when needed, and an understanding of the value of articulating their own progress—her students will struggle with owning their learning.

What Teachers Are Doing

What are other ways teachers have implemented this practice—"Each and every student is supported by **data** that is used to **monitor current understanding** and **adjust as needed**"—as they offer support for developing student ownership?

Take this example from a ninth-grade French teacher: "During an observation debrief, it was brought to my attention that I asked really good questions to monitor student understanding throughout the lesson. But it was also pointed out that I usually only called on one or two students to respond. I needed to find ways to monitor the understanding of all my students. I have since incorporated more student-to-student conversations. I will pose my question, give students time to think, and then have them discuss it with a peer. I try to listen in on as many conversations as I can. I then randomly call on a few students. I also ask if any partners were unable to answer. Not only do I get a sense of the entire class's preparedness to move on, but my students are given more opportunities to talk in French."

Take this example from a fifth-grade math teacher: "When I plan my lessons, I know my students need practice to build fluency and automaticity with the skills. I may have twenty computation problems ready for them to practice. But if I see after ten that they have it, with fluency, I don't have them keep going. It is not about getting through all the problems. It is about getting through the learning. When we have achieved that, I adjust and move on."

Take this example from a kindergarten teacher: "Before I move students on to independent practice, I have them self-assess. A *1* means they are ready to practice and could help a friend if needed. A *2* means they are ready to practice but may need some help. A *3* means they need more help before they practice. The '3' students stay with me, and we review the skill. The '2' students get started and can ask a '1' student if needed or come join my '3' group if they get stuck. The other students begin their practice. This flexible grouping technique allows me to easily adjust based on my students' needs."

What Students Are Saying

What do students say about this practice—"Each and every student is supported by **data** that is used to **monitor current understanding** and **adjust as needed**"—and its support for the ownership of their learning?

Take this example from a fourth grader: "My teacher is always asking us what we know and don't know. He tries different ways to make sure we understand. This has shown me that I have a say in my learning and that he really listens to us. It also taught me that I need to be able to do this for myself. I need to try different ways to learn if one way doesn't work for me."

Take this example from a middle school student: "Mrs. Crabapple, my history teacher, tells us stuff in many different ways. I like when she explains it to me. I like listening to her talk. Even when she is showing us a picture or a drawing, it doesn't make as much sense as when she then explains it. She tells me I'm good at listening and that this is one way I learn well. When I really think about my other classes, I realize that I learn best when I can hear what I am supposed to do. My mom says this means I'm an auditory learner."

Strategic Learning Practice, Assessment 3

Each and Every Student Is Supported by Data That Is Used to Differentiate Based on Predetermined Student Needs

In order for students to own their learning in regard to assessment, each and every student must be able to answer the following questions:

▸ What specific areas of need do you have?

▸ What supports might you need from the teacher?

▸ What strategies might you use to continue learning?

In order for teachers to develop students who own their learning in regard to assessment, it is imperative that teachers support students with practices that are strategically implemented on a daily basis. This requires a focus on those practices that Swanson and Hoskyn (1998) and Dunn, Griggs, Olson, Beasley, and Gorman (1995) show increase the opportunities for learning by increasing the opportunities for student ownership. Strategic Learning Practice, Assessment 3, states: "Each and every student is supported by **data** that is used to **differentiate** based on **predetermined student needs**."

First, let's define each aspect of this practice.

Data is any information that is gathered to indicate if the student has any specific learning concerns.

Differentiate is the action of the teacher to adapt or modify instructional materials, instructional strategies, or instructional processes in order to meet the specific needs of specific students so that the students can be supported in attaining the learning outcome.

Predetermined includes all the data a teacher is privy to before planning the lesson. This could include a student's IEP, English-learner status, previous assessment results, attendance, or anything pertinent in a student's record.

Student needs are those specific learning issues identified on an IEP, the language level and abilities of an English learner, misconceptions discovered from previous assessments, and gaps due to missed instructional time.

The Practice in Action

What does this practice—"Each and every student is supported by **data** that is used to **differentiate** based on **predetermined student needs**"—look like in a classroom at the highest level? You might walk into Mrs. Kumar's third-grade social studies class and hear the class discussing the learning outcome on the board: "Students will describe examples of human modification of the environment by creating a community change poster." You notice that there are visuals next to the words *human, modification, environment,* and *community.* You also notice the resource teacher, Miss Smith, working with students.

That is what the class discussed. But how much did the students understand? What happens when you ask them questions about their learning?

You: "What are you learning?"

Ana: "I am learning about how people make changes."

You: "What kind of changes do they make?"

Ana: "There was a farm here, but now it is a school. People did that."

You: "I see you have a chart next to you with pictures and words. Does that help you?"

Ana: "I am from El Salvador and still need to learn some new English words. Mrs. Kumar gives me this. If I see a word I don't know, the picture will help me. This is a hard word for me—*construction.* The picture helps me know it. Sometimes I know the word but not in English. Mrs. Kumar uses pictures a lot to help us. You can see some on the board."

Brian: "The pictures help me too. I have trouble remembering stuff. The pictures help me remember bigger words, or *academic words*, as Mrs. Kumar calls them."

You: "What other ways does Mrs. Kumar help you?"

Ana: "We sometimes get to show what we are doing. And we draw. I also talk with my friends a lot. We have to do that a lot. We also get help with reading. I can work with a friend who will read it with me and ask me questions. I get to answer and practice what he read before I try to read it."

Brian: "Mrs. Kumar gives me a sheet of paper that tells me the information I need to remember. Miss Smith sits with me and goes over this information until I can remember it. I also get to take the paper home and have my mom work with me. Mrs. Kumar and Miss Smith are nice."

You: "How will this help you with your community change poster?"

Ana: "I like art. Sometimes we get to pick what we do. I'm going to draw. I have learned lots of ways our community has changed. I am ready to show it on my poster. I will use the new words I have learned. It is good to keep learning new words."

Brian: "When I work with Miss Smith, she will help me find pictures for the information on my sheet. I can use these on my poster. The poster will help me remember things about communities."

Are you surprised that these students were so forthcoming about their specific needs? How did they gain the confidence to talk about the support they need? Let's talk to Mrs. Kumar.

"It is very important that each of my students understands their unique strengths and areas of need. We talk about the importance of understanding how we learn. They know that they can ask me, or Miss Smith, or one another for help. I remind them that asking for help when we struggle is something that we all do. In fact, I tell my students that, if they aren't struggling, then they aren't learning something new. We all struggle. This helps when I differentiate for different students. Everyone gets the help they need."

Mrs. Kumar used the Strategic Learning Practice, Assessment 3, as a frame to help her plan how she wanted to offer this support. This frame is flexible and fits the needs of both teachers and students. However, the following planning questions in table 3.8 helped her focus the support.

Questions to Guide Implementing Strategic Learning Practice, Assessment 3:

Each and every student is supported by data that is used to differentiate based on predetermined student needs.

Use these planning questions to focus your support.

	Notes
❑ What skill will my students learn, and how will they demonstrate they have learned it?	
❑ What current student data do I have to help plan the instruction?	
❑ What specific student needs must be addressed?	
❑ How will I differentiate instruction based on specific student needs?	
❑ How will I ensure the differentiated instruction directly aligns with the learning outcome?	
❑ How will I share this information with my students?	
❑ How will I check that my students understand their progress toward the goals of the unit or lesson?	
❑ How will my students understand that reflecting on the assessment of their learning supports ownership of their learning?	

Table 3.8: Questions to Guide Implementing Strategic Learning Practice, Assessment 3

Implementing the Practice

How did Mrs. Kumar use the questions in table 3.8 to help plan how she would offer support to her students? First, she had to determine the following:

▸ What skill will my students learn, and how will they demonstrate they have learned it?

Mrs. Kumar explains, "We are in our social studies unit on geography and human systems. The expectations for this standard call for students to describe examples of human modifications to the environment in the local community. I have a diverse group of learners in my classroom. I have four English-learner students, three mainstreamed special needs students, and an overall variety of learners throughout the class. I know that I need to take into account all my students' needs in order to meet the learning expectations. Not only do I need to provide the right supports, but I also need to make certain my students know what the supports are, why they are there, and how to access them as needed. For this lesson, there are many ways my students could demonstrate their understanding. I chose a poster because it will allow them to demonstrate learning at a variety of levels. Some will cut out pictures to show human modifications, some will draw and label, some will include a longer explanation. All students will share their poster and be required to use as much academic language as possible in explaining their learning."

Mrs. Kumar also had to determine the following:

▸ What current student data do I have to help plan the instruction?

▸ What specific student needs must be addressed?

Mrs. Kumar continues, "At the beginning of the year, I spent time reading each students' cumulative folder. I met with the special education teacher and reviewed my students' IEPs. I also reviewed my students' English-language-level data. This provided me with a baseline on each student. From there, I have carefully assessed them along the way to ensure I understand how they learn best, their areas of strength, and their areas of need. I have really amazing supports in my school, and I have relied on them to continually grow my repertoire of differentiated instructional strategies specific to different students' needs."

Mrs. Kumar had to ask herself the following questions:

▶ How will I differentiate instruction based on specific student needs?

▶ How will I ensure the differentiated instruction directly aligns with the learning outcome?

Mrs. Kumar says, "I have some students who are at the intermediate level in English and need more academic-language support. I have students with IEPs who have a variety of identified needs—including reading comprehension deficits, short-term memory issues, and auditory-processing concerns. I know I have to find alternative ways for all of these students to access key content. I know I need to chunk the content and provide multiple, varied opportunities for learning.

"At the beginning of this lesson, I introduced the objective. You will see that I included visual supports for any words that may be new to my students. After I read the objective, we discussed the words. From there I had the students choral read the objective a few times and then discuss it with their peers. I had my students seated in groups so there were always students of varying levels who could support one another.

"The next portion of the lesson was vocabulary. Vocabulary acquisition is a key skill that supports the English learners. It is also a key skill that supports struggling readers. I knew I needed to plan a variety of ways for them to understand these words. Some of the words we acted out, for others we used illustrations. We also made connections to words and concepts we already knew. This was just the beginning. We will use these words throughout the lesson in a variety of ways. For those students who need it, I have created a picture definition chart that they will keep on their desks throughout the unit.

"We also needed to read some text from a social studies book. I needed to plan how I would differentiate this to support all of my learners. We started with a whole-class discussion on what we thought the text would inform us about and why. I then had my students determine how they would access the text. Some read the text independently and completed a graphic organizer on the main idea and key details from the text. Some students listened to an audio recording of the text before reading. Some students worked with partners. And some students worked in a group with me. For today's lesson,

I predetermined who would work with me. My students understand their strengths and needs and can often make the choice themselves. They are quite good at making the right choices."

But Mrs. Kumar wanted to ensure that her students would be able to use the skills in a variety of situations. She wanted to help her students own this information so that she could increase the probability of their learning. She then had to determine the following:

- ▶ How will I share this information with my students?
- ▶ How will I check that my students understand their progress toward the goals of the unit or lesson?

Mrs. Kumar says, "Every class has students with unique strengths and areas of need. I think it is important that students understand what their strengths and needs are, as well as which ways they learn best. We constantly reflect on our learning. We discuss what we learned and how we learned it. We discuss ways we supported one another and learned from one another. I have a real community in this classroom. We continually discuss how we all learn differently and how, when we all work together, we all get smarter."

Mrs. Kumar was very interested in making sure her third graders understood the value of owning their own learning. Thus, she had to answer the following question:

- ▶ How will my students understand that reflecting on the assessment of their learning supports ownership of their learning?

Mrs. Kumar explains, "When we discuss as a class how we learn each day, we spend time talking about how that approach supports us. The strategies I employ most often with this class—audio and visual cues, total physical responses, chunking, modeling, collaboration, leveled materials, varied demonstrations of learning—are supportive for all learners. But this can't be information I keep to myself. I need my students to understand what approach is being utilized and why. They need to understand how they learn best. My students are getting stronger with this each day. They can tell you, more often than not, what their strengths are, where they need support, and what helps them learn best and why."

Teachers like Mrs. Kumar have realized that without this support—instruction differentiated to address specific learning needs—her students would struggle with owning their learning.

What Teachers Are Doing

What are other ways teachers have implemented this practice—"Each and every student is supported by **data** that is used to **differentiate** based on **predetermined student needs**"—as they offer support for developing student ownership?

Take this example from an elementary literacy coach: "I am a former special ed teacher and love helping my teachers with differentiated instruction. I remind them that we can differentiate instruction in four ways: through (1) content, (2) process, (3) product, or (4) learning environment; with the focus always on the needs of the individual learner."

Take this example from a middle school math teacher: "I used to think that just knowing the student was special education was enough because that usually meant, in my mind, that they were going to struggle. What else did I need to know, right? But then I began to read their IEPs and realized that each student has their own particular needs. Instead of adding more work to my planning, knowing this information actually made my planning much less daunting. Now I can differentiate for their specific needs and use their strengths as a jumping-off point."

Take this example from a seventh-grade physical education teacher: "Some days I get tired and find myself repeating things in a louder and slower voice thinking this will help the students get it. But I know that is not what they need. They need a different approach or sometimes just more time. It is important that I have preplanned a variety of approaches so I can pull a new one out as needed."

Take this example from an eleventh-grade English teacher: "We read a lot of complex texts in my class, and not all of my students can access these texts independently. I use chapter summaries that some students read before the lesson. This helps them make sense of the text as they read it. I also create key-word summaries of each chapter that we post throughout the novel. This helps my students who need it retain what has occurred so they can successfully move on in the text."

What Students Are Saying

What do students say about this practice—"Each and every student is supported by **data** that is used to **differentiate** based on **predetermined student needs**"—and its support for the ownership of their learning?

Take this example from a seventh grader: "At my school, we do student-led IEPs. This means I lead the meeting with my parents when we discuss my learning needs. This isn't easy to do, but I get a lot of help from my teachers. I have done this twice, and it has made me more aware of what I can do well and where I need help. It also gives me ideas about how I can help myself if no one is around or if they are busy. Before, when just my parents went, it felt secret and like I had done something wrong. All I knew is that I felt dumb. Now I feel like I can help myself."

Take this example from a high school English learner: "I know that if I want to get to college I need to work on my classes—like math, history, science—and also on my English. I know that I need more academic words that I can use. Whenever I hear a new word from the teacher, I write it down and try to use it all day."

Take this example from a fifth grader: "I have dyslexia. Reading has been hard for me. What I like about Mr. Ball is that he talks about my dyslexia with me. He tells me what we are doing to help me be a better reader. I know my other teachers try to help me, but they don't tell me what they are doing. It is easier when Mr. Ball just says that this science text has a lot of new words and that I am going to read the easier book first before I try the harder one. I like that we talk about it."

Assessment Reflection

How Well Do You Develop Students to Own How Well They Are Learning?

In this chapter, we have shown you what student ownership looks like in practice. We have shown you what it sounds like when students own their part in assessment. And we have given examples of how teachers have implemented these strategic learning practices in a variety of classrooms.

We have also explained the difference between a student who is simply *doing* or *understanding* assessment and one who is *owning* how well they are learning.

A student is *doing* when they can state how they finish the task in front of them.

A student is *understanding* when they can explain how they know they are learning.

A student is *owning* how well they are learning when they can articulate if they are learning or struggling and why, what to do if they are learning or struggling, and how assessing their learning helps them learn more.

Think of your students. Where do they fall on the doing-understanding-owning continuum? Think about the supports they need from you to develop student ownership. How often and to what degree do you offer these supports? In other words, what impact do you have on student ownership?

Remember that John Hattie (2011) said: "Such passion for evaluating impact is the single most critical lever for instructional excellence—accompanied by understanding this impact, and doing something in light of the evidence and understanding" (p. viii).

What follows are reflection activities that will help you determine your impact on student ownership—both areas of strength and areas of growth.

In order to develop student ownership, all student learning is driven by regular assessment that guides instructional decision-making. And, as always, your actions are key to the development of student ownership.

Reflect on Strategic Learning Practice, Assessment 1

Each and every student is supported by data that is used to monitor current understanding and provide feedback.

Consider how your students respond to the following questions:

▸ Are you learning, and how do you know?

▸ Are you struggling, and how do you know?

▸ How does checking for understanding and receiving feedback support your learning?

Think about your students' responses—remembering that your support is directly linked to developing student ownership—and use the following to help you reflect on the strengths and gaps of your support.

How often and how well do you offer these supports?

- Planned data checks are utilized to effectively monitor current student understanding of the learning outcomes.

- Direct and specific feedback affirms current understanding of the relevant standards and measurable and achievable learning outcomes.

- Direct and specific feedback clarifies or redirects current understanding and builds toward mastery of the relevant standards and measurable and achievable learning outcomes.

Table 3.9: Reflect on Strategic Learning Practice, Assessment 1

Reflect on Strategic Learning Practice, Assessment 2

Each and every student is supported by data that is used to monitor current understanding and adjust as needed.

Consider how your students respond to the following questions:

▸ Are you struggling, and how do you know?

▸ What supports might you need from the teacher?

▸ What strategies might you use to continue learning?

Think about your students' responses—remembering that your support is directly linked to developing student ownership—and use the following to help you reflect on the strengths and gaps of your support.

How often and how well do you offer these supports?

- Planned data checks are utilized to effectively monitor current student understanding of the learning outcomes.

- Information from data checks is used to consistently and effectively adjust instruction, building toward mastery of the relevant standards and measurable and achievable learning outcomes.

- Data is used to determine next steps, including reteaching.

- Data is used to determine next steps, including acceleration.

Table 3.10: Reflect on Strategic Learning Practice, Assessment 2

Reflect on Strategic Learning Practice, Assessment 3

Each and every student is supported by data that is used to differentiate based on predetermined student needs.

Consider how your students respond to the following questions:

▸ What specific areas of need do you have?

▸ What supports might you need from the teacher?

▸ What strategies might you use to continue learning?

Think about your students' responses—remembering that your support is directly linked to developing student ownership—and use the following to help you reflect on the strengths and gaps of your support.

How often and how well do you offer these supports?

- All differentiation is planned and meets the predetermined needs of the identified student or students.

- All differentiation aligns directly to and builds toward mastery of the relevant standards and measurable and achievable learning outcomes.

- Reflection on the purpose and value of specific differentiated supports is required of students.

Table 3.11: Reflect on Strategic Learning Practice, Assessment 3

4 CLIMATE
Developing Students to Own Their Role in the Class

For many teachers, climate means a well-behaved classroom. Students sit calmly, don't shout, and raise their hands when asked. For years this order and structure were the hallmarks of a well-run classroom. Students are often still graded on their social behavior. In fact, in many schools, students are given an academic grade based on their social behavior.

This approach to climate tends to focus on the actions of the teachers— their rules, their management policy, their ability to get kids to stay quietly in their seats. As teachers, we know how tiring this is. We need to flip this to focus on the actions of the students—*their* role in the class, *their* scholarly behaviors that support their learning, *their* willingness and ability to support others and their learning. Students need to go home more tired than the teacher. True student ownership begins when the teacher looks at climate from the point of view of the student.

Climate is defined as a student-centered environment that accelerates academic learning. This goes beyond a well-behaved classroom. We know that an out-of-control classroom has negative effects on learning. But the opposite is not true. A well-behaved classroom does not guarantee learning will occur. Students are more supported to own their learning when they understand their role in the academic classroom. The role of the student in this academic classroom is key. Their role is to actively pursue their own learning while respectfully, cooperatively, and collaboratively helping others actively pursue their learning.

The Imperatives of Ownership of Climate

To develop student ownership, several things are imperative: It is imperative for students to know and be able to articulate their role in the classroom. It is imperative for students to know that the group of students as a whole is smarter than any one individual student. It is imperative for students to articulate their role in building a respectful, cooperative, and collaborative classroom. It is imperative for students to understand the value of learning in a classroom that recognizes and promotes all students. It is imperative for students to honor risk taking and understand how struggling is a crucial part of the learning process—for them and their classmates. It is imperative for students to support each other in the learning endeavor. It is imperative for students to value cooperative and collaborative group work as a support of their own learning.

Table 4.1 provides some helpful indicators that reveal when students are taking ownership of their learning.

Indicators of Student Ownership of Climate

Each and every student is able to articulate:

- what they are learning and how they will demonstrate they have learned it,
- their role in the class,
- their role in recognizing and promoting others,
- the scholarly behaviors that support their learning,
- how they support others in their learning,
- how they take academic risks,
- the value of taking academic risks,
- how they work with other students,
- the value of working with other students,
- how teamwork supports all students in achieving mastery of the learning, and
- why articulating these aspects of climate helps them own their learning.

Table 4.1: Indicators of Student Ownership of Climate

Students who are part of this class are involved in a community that invites students to learn. William Purkey (1992) defines this type of class as one based on "Invitational Learning."

"The model is based on four propositions:

- trust, in that we need to convince not coerce others to engage in what we would like them to consider worthwhile activities;

- respect, in that we adopt caring and appropriate behaviors when treating others;

- optimism, in seeking the untapped potential and uniqueness in others;

- intentionality, in which we create programs by people designed to invite learning." (p. 8)

Students are at the center of this class, and they own their role in the learning.

Putting Student Ownership into Practice

But what does student ownership look like in practice? What does it sound like when a student owns their part in climate? What is the difference between a student who is simply *doing* or *understanding* classroom climate and one who is *owning* their role in the class?

A student is *doing* when they can state the rules in the classroom.

A student is *understanding* when they can explain how a respectful, cooperative, and collaborative class supports their learning.

A student is *owning* their role in the class when they can articulate their role in a respectful, cooperative, and collaborative environment, how scholarly behaviors support their own learning, and how they can develop this environment and these behaviors for future use.

The tables that follow—table 4.2, table 4.3, table 4.4, and table 4.5—present some examples of what this looks and sounds like on a continuum of doing-understanding-owing in a variety of content areas and grade levels, particularly when we ask the question, "What is your role in the class?"

Possible responses on the continuum from second grade students in history/social studies when asked,

"What is your role in the class?"

"The teacher tells me what I need to do, and I do it."

"I can talk to my friends or the teacher if I need help with my work."

"I have to make and share my poster, but before I do, I get to practice with my team. This helps me make sure I am ready, and my work is good. I also get ideas from them when they share. It is kind of scary to share with the whole class, but it is easier when I practice first and know my team is there for me. We know that we all get a little scared, but watching my friends do the same things makes it less scary."

DOING   UNDERSTANDING   OWNING

Table 4.2: Student Ownership Continuum, History/Social Studies, Grade 2

Possible responses on the continuum from third grade students in science when asked,

"What is your role in the class?"

"We have rules we have to follow so we don't get in trouble."

"Sometimes we get to work together. We are working on a weather chart. I'm the timekeeper for the group."

"We are learning about weather. We gathered data on each season. Once we had the data we shared it and looked for patterns. My team helped me make sure my data was right. They saw some patterns I didn't even see. I helped them, too. What we learn from one season will help us with others. We will work together and give each other ideas to help make our data better."

DOING   UNDERSTANDING   OWNING

Table 4.3: Student Ownership Continuum, Science, Grade 3

Possible responses on the continuum from sixth grade students in math when asked,

"What is your role in the class?"

"We are learning to identify equivalent expressions. It can be confusing, so we work in groups to help each other out. We get to ask each other questions and talk about our mistakes. We have to decide as a team which expressions are equivalent and which ones are not. We have to tell why we know we are right. Our teacher makes us talk it through. This helps us practice and learn. I wish all of my classrooms let us work together."

"When the bell rings we get right to work. We do a starter activity to remind us what we are learning. My job is to learn."

"We sit in groups and work together."

DOING   **UNDERSTANDING**   **OWNING**

Table 4.4: Student Ownership Continuum, Math, Grade 6

Possible responses on the continuum from eleventh grade students in English-language arts when asked,

"What is your role in the class?"

"We are giving speeches on the Constitution. We need to present an organized speech that the audience can easily follow. I don't like presenting in front of the class. But I know that the more familiar I am with my speech and the more I practice it, the better I will be. I will present to my partner to see if she can easily follow the speech. If she can't, the presentation is not strong enough. The more we help each other, the more confident we are."

"We will give our presentation, and the class will give us a score on how we did."

"We have a syllabus that shows what is due. I meet the deadlines."

DOING   **UNDERSTANDING**   **OWNING**

Table 4.5: Student Ownership Continuum, English-Language Arts, Grade 11

Moving to Student Ownership

What can a teacher do to move a student toward owning their learning? Student ownership is best defined as a mindset. Students who know they have the authority, capacity, and responsibility to own their learning possess an ownership mindset. Thus, to move a student, the teacher must delegate the authority, build the capacity, and give the responsibility to each and every student.

How does a teacher do this? They must model the thinking behind the ownership and explicitly teach the skills of ownership. This takes planning. In order for students to answer the questions posed earlier—"What is my role in the class?", "How will I help others in their learning?", and "How will I take risks in my learning?"—teachers must be strategic in the practices they use to increase learning.

While there are hundreds of actions a teacher must take in a day, we will focus on those three practices in climate that research shows increase the opportunities for learning—by increasing the opportunities for student ownership.

Teachers must strategically decide when to offer the following three learning practices:

- **Strategic Learning Practice, Climate 1:** Each and every student is supported by a respectful academic environment that recognizes and promotes scholarly behaviors.

- **Strategic Learning Practice, Climate 2:** Each and every student is supported by a cooperative academic environment that encourages risk taking.

- **Strategic Learning Practice, Climate 3:** Each and every student is supported by a collaborative academic environment that enhances student productivity.

In the following sections, we will clearly define each learning practice, describe what implementation looks and sounds like in the classroom, share teacher planning questions, offer examples of how students have been supported with these learning practices in a variety of content areas and grade levels, and explain how these practices directly lead to increased student ownership.

Strategic Learning Practice, Climate 1

Each and Every Student Is Supported by a Respectful Academic Environment That Recognizes and Promotes Scholarly Behaviors

In order for students to own their learning in regard to climate, each and every student must be able to answer the following questions:

▸ What is your role in the class?

▸ How do you recognize and promote others?

▸ Which scholarly behaviors support your learning?

In order for teachers to develop students who own their learning in regard to climate, it is imperative that teachers support students with practices that are strategically implemented on a daily basis. This requires a focus on those practices that Cornelius-White (2007) and Haertel and Walberg (1980) show increase the opportunities for learning by increasing the opportunities for student ownership. Strategic Learning Practice, Climate 1, states: "Each and every student is supported by a **respectful academic environment** that **recognizes** and **promotes scholarly behaviors**."

First, let's define each aspect of this practice.

Being **respectful** is the cornerstone attribute of an effective and efficient classroom. This means that teachers and students honor and accept each other as scholars and unique individuals with specific learning strengths and needs.

The **academic environment** is both the physical space and the mental attitude of the classroom. These spaces are set up and organized to support teaching and learning. The attitude is student-centered—the focus is on the scholar, their needs, and their behaviors.

Recognizes refers to the intentional acknowledgment of scholarly behaviors, specific and public.

Promotes refers to the intentional acknowledgment of scholarly behaviors to nurture and advance the learning.

Scholarly behaviors include those actions that support learning—such as perseverance, effort, resourcefulness, self-management, reflection, precision, and active participation—and lead to increased academic ownership.

The Practice in Action

What does this practice—"Each and every student is supported by a **respectful academic environment** that **recognizes** and **promotes scholarly behaviors**"—look like in a classroom at the highest level? You might walk into Miss Kocourek's kindergarten class and read the following learning outcome on the chart: "I will identify key details by asking and answering questions about the book *A Cold Land*."

That is what you read. But what happens when you talk to the students about their learning?

You: "What are you learning?"

Student: "I am learning about details. When an author writes a book, they include lots of details."

You: "What are details?"

Student: "They are things the author writes so you know what it is all about. Our book is about a cold place. There are lots of details about the place."

You: "I see you are talking with your partner. How does that help you learn?"

Student: "I am asking her questions about the book, and she has to tell me the answer. Then she gets to ask me a question."

You: "How do you know what questions to ask?"

Student: "We have to use our book. See, it says animals live here, and then there are animal pictures and words. I can ask her what animals live here, and she has to answer. It has to be a detail from our book."

You: "How does working together help you both learn?"

Student: "We get to practice together. And if she gives me a good answer, I tell her good job. We also have to tell how it was a good job. I told her she did a good job telling me *penguin* because she used the picture in the book. She told me she liked my question because it was about animals, and she likes animals."

You: "That's nice that you say kind things to each other. Do you do that a lot?"

Student: "Yes. Miss K says we have to help each other and tell each other when we see that we are doing good things for learning. Then we get to tell everyone else. It's fun to share."

You: "What kind of good things for learning do you usually see?"

Student: "I see people share. I see people try hard. I see people being good listeners. I see people helping one another. This is what scholars do. Miss K taught us that word. It means we are in school to learn. If we do any of these things, we get a 'Good Scholar' sticker to wear."

Are you wondering how the student was able to answer your questions so clearly and with such confidence? Let's ask Miss Kocourek.

"Kindergarteners come to me with a range of social skills. I know that I need to spend a lot of energy throughout the school year preparing my children to be academic students. They need to learn how to be a productive member of a class—that is, working hard as an individual scholar as well as helping others do the same. With a class full or five- and six-year-olds, I need them all working together."

Miss Kocourek used the Strategic Learning Practice, Climate 1, as a frame to help her plan how she wanted to offer this support. This frame is flexible and fits the needs of both teachers and students. However, the following planning questions in table 4.6 helped her focus the support.

Questions to Guide Implementing Strategic Learning Practice, Climate 1:

Each and every student is supported by a respectful academic environment that recognizes and promotes scholarly behaviors.

Use these planning questions to focus your support.

	Notes
❑ What skill will my students learn and how will they demonstrate they have learned it?	
❑ How will I ensure an academic environment that is student-centered?	
❑ What opportunities will I plan for respectful interactions— teacher to student, student to teacher, student to student?	
❑ What opportunities will I plan to allow for recognition and promotion of students and their behaviors?	
❑ What opportunities will I plan to support scholarly behaviors?	
❑ How will I share this information with my students?	
❑ How will I check that my students understand the impact of scholarly behaviors on their learning?	
❑ How will my students understand that reflecting on their scholarly behaviors supports ownership of their learning?	

Table 4.6: Questions to Guide Implementing Strategic Learning Practice, Climate 1

Implementing the Practice

How did Miss Kocourek use the questions in table 4.6 to help plan how she would offer support to her students? First, she had to determine the following:

> ▶ What skill will my students learn and how will they demonstrate they have learned it?

Miss Kocourek explains, "We are in a unit that focuses on reading informational texts. My students will be 'writing' an informative text at the end of the unit. 'Writing' for many of my students still means drawing and labeling information. But everyone will have to include a main idea and key details. Our reading skills will help our writing skills. Today I am focusing on standard K.RI.1: 'With prompting and support, ask and answer questions about key details in a text.' We have worked on this skill quite a bit this year. The students will continue this skill in first grade, but without prompting and support. Today I want them to practice applying the skill with a book we have read together and they have read on their own."

Miss Kocourek then had to ask the following question of herself:

> ▶ How will I ensure an academic environment that is student-centered?

Miss Kocourek says, "Kindergarten is a huge year of growth. For many of my children, this is their first school experience. I only have a handful of them that attended preschool. This means I set the stage for their academic success. They must understand that school is about learning and growing every day. They must understand that they have a role in the classroom for their own learning and for the other students. I don't ever tell my students they are smart. I make sure to tell them the behaviors they displayed that will lead to growth as a scholar. I tell them that I will ask a lot of them, but I will always make sure they are successful if they try. In kindergarten, this is not as hard as in upper grades because they believe you and are inclined to take risks. If I set a strong foundation with them, they will carry this scholarly attitude forward each year."

Miss Kocourek then had to determine the following:

> ▶ What opportunities will I plan for respectful interactions—teacher to student, student to teacher, student to student?

▸ What opportunities will I plan to allow for recognition and promotion of students and their behaviors?

    ▸ What opportunities will I plan to support scholarly behaviors?

Miss Kocourek goes on, "For this lesson, the students are working with a partner to ask and answer questions about details from their book. I know I want to intentionally continue developing a supportive learning environment. My children must not only ask and answer questions but they must also provide feedback on scholarly behaviors. I have listed them on this chart, and we discuss them every day. Today's lesson lent itself well to practicing this and everyone feels successful. The child getting the compliment is recognized for their behavior. The one giving the compliment is reminded of the behavior."

But Miss Kocourek wanted to help her students own this information so that she could increase the probability of their learning. She then had to answer the following questions:

    ▸ How will I share this information with my students?

    ▸ How will I check that my students understand the impact of scholarly behaviors on their learning?

Miss Kocourek says, "When we review our learning each day, we refer to our scholarly behaviors chart. We talk about how those behaviors help us as learners. We share scholarly behaviors we observed and scholarly behaviors we displayed. I make sure I model how to give and receive positive feedback. During our review, I make sure it is not just me talking but that the students talk to one another about the learning and how their actions led to greater learning. One thing I love about kindergartners is that they love to talk about themselves, and they are incredibly generous with compliments. I just make sure it is all focused on academics and scholarly behaviors."

Miss Kocourek is committed to ensuring that her students understand the value of owning their own learning. Thus, she has to determine the following:

    ▸ How will my students understand that reflecting on their scholarly behaviors supports ownership of their learning?

Miss Kocourek explains, "Beyond reflecting on our learning in the classroom, we talk about what it means outside of the classroom. The children are able to make connections to their sports activities and home life. They can also tell you how these scholarly behaviors are important in every class. When they return, say from physical education, we talk about what they learned and what scholarly behaviors they used."

Teachers like Miss Kocourek have realized that without this support—respect for everyone in the classroom; public recognition and promotion of each student's effort; and a focus on effective scholarly behaviors—her students would struggle with owning their learning.

What Teachers Are Doing

What are other ways teachers have implemented this practice—"Each and every student is supported by a **respectful academic environment** that **recognizes** and **promotes scholarly behaviors**"—as they offer support for developing student ownership?

Take this example from a geometry teacher and physical education coach: "As a coach, I am constantly telling my team when they are doing well. They need this encouragement if they are going to get better. I run alongside them and tell them specifically what they were doing well, especially when it is something they just were beginning to perfect. It never occurred to me to do the same thing in my geometry class. I don't run up and down the rows, but I am more open about giving encouragement to my math students. This made me realize that good teaching is about good coaching."

Take this example from a middle school industrial arts teacher: "I have always encouraged my students, but it was a bit superficial. I thought they knew what I was referring to when I would tell them good job. Once when I told a student good job about how he was sawing the 2 x 4 by using gloves and goggles, he turned to his friend and said, 'See, I told you it was better to choose the 2 x 4.' He had missed the point. That made me realize that I needed to be specific."

Take this example from a high school history teacher: "I was in a workshop, and they used a recognition strategy. Whenever someone shared their learning, the speaker would acknowledge it by saying, 'Thank you for sharing, James. Let's give James two snaps and a clap.' I thought, 'There is no way my high school students will go for this. They will think it is so corny.' But I gave it a try. To my surprise, they loved it. I think it is such a simple way to acknowledge effort and the sharing of thinking and learning. When they share, it doesn't have to be right, it just promotes always trying. It has now become just what we do in my classes."

What Students Are Saying

What do students say about this practice—"Each and every student is supported by a **respectful academic environment** that **recognizes** and **promotes scholarly behaviors**"—and its support for the ownership of their learning?

Take this example from a seventh grader: "I like when my teacher, Mr. Balsamo, talks about the behaviors that make someone smarter. This makes me think that I can do almost anything if I put my mind to it. I used to think that a person was either good or bad at something. For example, math is hard for me. But there are things I can do for myself to help me learn better. These are the scholarly behaviors Mr. Balsamo is talking about."

Take this example from a fifth grader: "My teacher has a chart on the wall that tells about scholarly behaviors. Each month we get to choose a behavior we want to focus on. At the end of each week, we write at least three ways we exhibited the behavior and how it helped us learn. If we do that, we get a free homework pass. I wish all my teachers did this because I do most of them all of the time. They really help me in learning."

Strategic Learning Practice, Climate 2

Each and Every Student Is Supported by a Cooperative Academic Environment That Encourages Risk Taking

In order for students to own their learning in regard to climate, each and every student must be able to answer the following questions:

▸ How do you support others in their learning?

▸ How do you take academic risks?

▸ What is the value of taking academic risks?

In order for teachers to develop students who own their learning in regard to climate, it is imperative that teachers support students with practices that are strategically implemented on a daily basis. This requires a focus on those practices that Stevens and Slavin (1990) and Huang (1991) show increase the opportunities for learning by increasing the opportunities for student ownership. Strategic Learning Practice, Climate 2, states: "Each and every student is supported by a **cooperative academic environment** that **encourages risk taking**."

First, let's define each aspect of this practice.

Cooperative describes the mutual assistance of individuals as they join together to achieve a common learning outcome. In student vernacular, it means that the people in the classroom (teachers and students) have one another's backs and support one another's learning successes.

The **academic environment** is both the physical space and the mental attitude of the classroom. These spaces are set up and organized to support teaching and learning. The attitude is student-centered—the focus is on the scholar, their needs, and their behaviors.

Encourages means to give support, confidence, and hope to the learner and their efforts.

Risk taking is the act of taking a chance, knowing failure may occur on the first attempt, in order to achieve an academic goal that presents a challenge to the learner. Risk takers know that true learning is about change and that change takes effort; they also willingly accept the possibility of struggle.

The Practice in Action

What does this practice—"Each and every student is supported by a **cooperative academic environment** that **encourages risk taking**"—look like in a classroom at the highest level? You might walk into Señor Mayorga's seventh-grade Spanish class and read the following learning outcome: "Students will apply community and directional words in order to ask and answer questions in Spanish using their community map."

That is what you read. But what happens when you talk to the students about their learning?

You: "What are you learning?"

Student: "I am learning to apply community and directional words in Spanish. I have to be able to give directions to different places and answer questions in Spanish using our community map."

You: "Tell me about your community map."

Student: "We worked in a group to make this. Señor Mayorga told us we had to create and label a map that included at least fifteen community places and eight streets. We had to use as many of our vocabulary words in our map as we could."

You: "How did you support one another while making the map?"

Student: "We worked well together. We do a lot of group work in this class. At the beginning of the year, we got to decide the rules of teamwork. We have practiced them. We also do a teamwork reflection and set individual and class goals for improvement. Our class goal right now is to support and encourage one another. We are trying to use as much Spanish as we can when we talk to each other. This can get frustrating sometimes because we don't know the right word. But we support one another to figure it out. We know we are all learning Spanish. If we get stuck, we can use English, but if it is a word we know in Spanish, our team has to encourage us to use it."

You: "What if one student didn't do any work?"

Student: "Well, I guess that could happen. But my group decided on everyone's job. But the map is not the most important part of what we have to do. The map is just the more fun part. We have to use our map to tell one another how to get from one place to another. So we are practicing asking and answering questions." The student points to a pair of students sitting at the next table. "He just asked her, *¿Cómo voy al banco desde la escuela?* That means: 'How do I go to the bank from the school?' Now she has to use the map to tell him."

You: "Your Spanish is really good."

Student: "Thanks. But I am still learning. I wasn't always this good, but I keep practicing. I like learning it, but it can be hard. The words don't always come easily, and I forget some of the rules. Señor Mayorga tells us we need to hear and use Spanish a lot to get better. That means a lot of talking and listening. He says that speaking in Spanish can feel uncomfortable but that we have to take the risk if we want to get better. Sometimes I don't want to say something because I know it will be wrong. But he tells us to try and not worry. When we talk to one another, we can help one another make our Spanish better."

You: "How can taking risks help you?"

Student: "If I don't try, I won't get better."

You: "How will you know when you have learned this today?"

Student: "When we think our group is ready, we raise our hands. Then Señor Mayorga will come to our table to test us. He can ask any of us any question, and we have to be able to answer. He will ask everyone a question. We will get our own grade, but we will also get a team grade on how well we support one another. So we have to help one another to make sure everyone is ready. If it doesn't go well, we get to practice some more and then call Señor Mayorga back."

Are you wondering how the student was able to answer your questions so clearly and with such confidence? Let's ask Señor Mayorga.

"First-year Spanish is usually my favorite class. The students are all new to learning a foreign language. Learning Spanish includes a lot of talking and listening to something they don't understand, so it can feel uncomfortable. I need to make certain I set up a class where everyone feels safe to take chances. Since they have to do so much speaking and listening, they have to work together a lot. I have to have an atmosphere of support, and our class goal is to make sure everyone feels comfortable to take risks—and they take them."

Señor Mayorga used the Strategic Learning Practice, Climate 2, as a frame to help him plan how he wanted to offer this support. This frame is flexible and fits the needs of both teachers and students. However, the following planning questions in table 4.7 helped him focus the support.

Questions to Guide Implementing Strategic Learning Practice, Climate 2:

Each and every student is supported by a cooperative academic environment that encourages risk taking.

Use these planning questions to focus your support.

	Notes
❑ What skill will my students learn, and how will they demonstrate they have learned it?	
❑ How will I ensure an academic environment?	
❑ What opportunities will I plan for authentic cooperation?	
❑ What opportunities will I plan to allow for cooperative behaviors?	
❑ What opportunities will I plan to encourage risk taking?	
❑ How will I share this information with my students?	
❑ How will I check that my students understand the impact of scholarly behaviors on their learning?	
❑ How will my students understand that reflecting on their scholarly behaviors supports ownership of their learning?	

Table 4.7: Questions to Guide Implementing Strategic Learning Practice, Climate 2

Implementing the Practice

How did Señor Mayorga use the questions in table 4.7 to help plan how he would offer support to his students? First, he had to determine the following:

▶ What skill will my students learn, and how will they demonstrate they have learned it?

Señor Mayorga says, "We are working on our unit on community. We have been learning community, location, and directional words and how to use them while asking directions. Today's lesson is an application of vocabulary and asking and answering questions in the proper tense. Rather than giving a traditional written test, I decided to do something that would ensure more speaking and listening. I don't want my students memorizing words and grammar rules. They need to authentically apply the skills as frequently as possible. Working in cooperative groups allows them to practice with their peers. They can make mistakes together and help one another work on their fluency. The group test will let me know where each student is and what additional instructional supports they still need."

Señor Mayorga then had to ask himself the following question:

▶ How will I ensure an academic environment?

Señor Mayorga explains, "In a class where risk taking is a must, I know I have to have a strong cooperative environment. I expect the behaviors of basic manners, but this goes beyond those. I need to make sure we have the behaviors of learning. My students have to not only understand how they support one another but why. I begin each school year by defining what these behaviors look like and sound like and explaining their value."

Next, Señor Mayorga needed to think about the following questions:

▶ What opportunities will I plan for authentic cooperation?

▶ What opportunities will I plan to allow for cooperative behaviors?

Señor Mayorga continues, "One behavior we discuss over and over is cooperation. Once we understand what we mean by *cooperation*, I let the students define what they will do, specifically, to ensure we have it. I have to put it on them. I cannot demand cooperation. They have to want it and own it. But it can't just be a conversation. I have to plan lots of lessons that require it. This allows us to practice and grow. For this lesson, I let them decide how to approach the mapmaking. I enjoyed seeing that different groups did it differently, but they all built a map that met the requirements. The map was not crucial to the learning, but it reinforced the vocabulary with the labels, it gave them a chance to own their roles in working as a cooperative group, and it was fun for them."

Señor Mayorga then had to determine the following:

▸ What opportunities will I plan to encourage risk taking?

Señor Mayorga says, "Learning a new language is all about risk taking. My students understand that there will be lots of struggle and sometimes frustration in this class. They are used to being able to communicate their ideas easily in English. It is easy to give up in Spanish and just revert back to English. But they know that with the risk comes the reward. I plan each lesson to ensure they have opportunities for successful practice on previous learning as well as new learning that will require work and challenges. They hear themselves and one another getting better and better."

But Señor Mayorga wanted to help his students own this information so that he could increase the probability of their learning. He therefore had to determine the answers to the following questions:

▸ How will I share this information with my students?

▸ How will I check that my students understand the impact of scholarly behaviors on their learning?

Señor Mayorga goes on, "As I said, we start each year defining what cooperation is and what it will look and sound like in our class. My students understand that learning a new language can only happen if you use it as much as possible. This means we have to talk and listen to one another. If they only talked and listened to me that would give them very little practice. They have to rely on one another. And not just as sounding board, but as fellow learners. This means encouraging and supporting one another. It means understanding that we are all learners. I make sure we not only congratulate one another for our efforts but that we also tell one another how those efforts made us individually and collectively smarter. My students are getting really good at this type of feedback. They really have one another's backs. I'm proud of them."

Señor Mayorga is committed to ensuring that his students understand the value of owning their own learning. Thus, he had to determine the following:

▸ How will my students understand that reflecting on their scholarly behaviors supports ownership of their learning?

Señor Mayorga explains, "At the end of each week, we review what was learned and how they feel they are doing. We discuss what they did specifically to support their own learning. We also discuss what they did to support someone else's learning. Some of their answers amaze me. One student last week said that he knows he will get an A in Spanish this year. I asked him why he was so confident. He said because he knew that if that is what he wants to do, everyone in this class would make sure he did it."

Teachers like Señor Mayorga have realized that without this support—a student-centered academic environment, cooperative activities that allow for students to encourage one another's behaviors and efforts, and words and actions that allow for academic risk taking—his students will struggle with owning their learning.

What Teachers Are Doing

What are other ways teachers have implemented this practice—"Each and every student is supported by a **cooperative academic environment** that **encourages risk taking**"—as they offer support for developing student ownership?

Take this example from a fourth-grade teacher: "Taking risks is hard for kids if they don't have the right mindset. I have a bulletin board dedicated to the growth mindset. I've posted a comparison between negative and positive mindsets. I teach my students to listen to one another and support them with a growth mindset. For example, if they hear a friend say, 'I can't do this,' then they need to tell them, 'Come on, take a risk, you can do it.' If they hear, 'I give up,' then tell them, 'Let's try some of the strategies we've learned.' If they hear, 'This is too hard,' then tell them, 'It may take some time, but you can do it. You can learn anything you want to.' If they hear, 'I made a mistake,' then tell them, 'Mistakes make us learn better.'"

Take this example from a high school social studies teacher: "I start every lesson by introducing the objective. We read and discuss what skill we will be learning and how we will demonstrate we have learned it. I then ask students to raise their hand if they can do the demonstration of learning right now. Typically no hands go up. Then I ask them if they are confident they will be able to demonstrate the learning by the end of the class, and all hands go up. When I first started doing this, I would have only a smattering of hands go up. But they quickly realized we would "get there." Now, not only are they confident that we will get there, but they also hold me and their peers to it. If they are getting lost or confused, they will let me know that learning is not happening. If someone gets off task or needs help, they help them. It has changed my class from a teacher teaching individual students to a "we" class. We all know where we are going, and we all work together to get there."

What Students Are Saying

What do students say about this practice—"Each and every student is supported by a **cooperative academic environment** that **encourages risk taking**"—and its support for the ownership of their learning?

Take this example from a fourth grader: "My teacher taught us how to help one another when we are having trouble. I like talking like the teacher. When my friend says, 'This is good enough,' I tell them, 'Are you sure? Is it really your best work? Let's see if we can make it better.' Talking this way makes me feel helpful."

Take this example from a high school senior: "I think one of the best things I learned in high school was about the growth mindset in my psychology class. It never occurred to me that I was in control of how I approached my own education. I can look at something negatively—'I can't do that, so I won't do that.' Or I can look at it positively with a growth mindset—'I can't do that now, but with help and perseverance, I will be able to do it.' This mindset will help me with all of the challenges I'm going to face in college."

Take this example from a high school biology student: "We work in cooperative groups a lot in my biology class. Last week, we were studying the digestive system. Our group had to work together to dissect a rat and to identify and place a pin in any organ that was part of the digestive system. As a team, we had to agree that we'd identified all of the organs correctly. From there, we each had to be able to name the identified organ and state its primary role in the digestive system. We worked together to make certain all information was accurate and each person could correctly name each pinned organ and its role. Once we were ready, we presented to the teacher. She came to the lab table and randomly called one of us and pointed to a pin. You had to correctly name the organ and its role. We got both an individual and a group grade. I like working as a team because we all help one another, but I don't get a bad grade if someone doesn't try."

Strategic Learning Practice, Climate 3

Each and Every Student Is Supported by a Collaborative Academic Environment That Enhances Student Productivity

In order for students to own their learning in regard to climate, each and every student must be able to answer the following questions:

▸ How do you work with other students?

▸ What is the value of working as a team?

▸ How does working on a team support your learning?

In order for teachers to develop students who own their learning in regard to climate, it is imperative that teachers support students with practices that are strategically implemented on a daily basis. This requires a focus on those practices that Stevens and Slavin (1990), Marzano (2000), and Haertel and Walberg (1980) show increase the opportunities for learning by increasing the opportunities for student ownership. Strategic Learning Practice, Climate 3, states: "Each and every student is supported by a **collaborative academic environment** that **enhances student productivity**."

First, let's define each aspect of this practice.

Collaborative comes from the Latin word *laborare*, which means "to work." In other words, students are working alongside other students to achieve or produce something.

The **academic environment** is both the physical space and the mental attitude of the classroom. These spaces are set up and organized to support teaching and learning. The attitude is student-centered—the focus is on the scholar, their needs, and their behaviors.

Enhances means to intensify, increase, or further improve the quality of the learning.

Student productivity is the effectiveness of the effort of individuals as they are learning. Via a collaborative approach, individual learning is increased.

The Practice in Action

What does this practice—"Each and every student is supported by a **collaborative academic environment** that **enhances student productivity**"—look like in a classroom at the highest level? You might walk into Mr. Schoonover's fourth-grade science period. On the science bulletin board, you will find information regarding the unit on energy, the final project for the unit (an informative and explanatory essay), and the current lesson outcome. The outcome reads: "Students will apply scientific ideas to design, test, and refine a device that converts energy from one form to another."

That is a lot of information for a fourth grader to understand. What do they tell you when you ask them questions about their learning in science?

You: "What are you learning?"

Student: "We are learning how energy is converted from one form to another. We have been studying this for the past two weeks. Today we will begin our experiment. As a team, we will have to design, build, test, and refine a machine that converts at least two different types of energy. See, it's all here in our project instructions. The fun part is that we are going to be working on this in teams."

You: "How do you work with other students?"

Student: "I think I do a pretty good job. Mr. Schoonover gives us projects that are too hard to do on our own. We have to work together. This means we all have to help, share ideas, and do our best. We also get a score on how we work as a team. Because I know what is on the collaboration behaviors rubric, I can make sure I do all of that."

You: "How does working on a team support your learning?"

Student: "It really helps me understand the science better. Because I had to talk about and explain what I knew about energy, it helped me remember more. We had to review a lot of information from before, and by working together, it showed me that I knew more than I thought. But that's science. Team projects also help me learn how to work with others. This is something Mr. Schoonover says all scientists do in their jobs, so I want to be really good at this. I am good at sharing ideas, but I need some help on listening to others and not getting defensive when they don't agree with me. But the more I work with my classmates, the more I realize that the disagreement usually leads to a better solution. So, I am open to the idea that my team might not agree the first time but that we will have a better machine because of it."

Are you wondering how the student was able to answer your questions so clearly and with such confidence? Let's ask Mr. Schoonover.

"It is clear that today's students don't need me for accessing science content. They can go to the internet and find out anything they want about energy. But what they can't do is understand, practice, and apply the scientific thinking that is actually needed to solve problems in the twenty-first century. They need me for that. My job is to show them how a scientist thinks and works. Most scientists today work together and push one another's thinking—challenging and arguing to get at stronger solutions. I need my students to not only know this but to experience it firsthand. That's why collaboration is such a large part of my classroom."

Mr. Schoonover used the Strategic Learning Practice, Climate 3, as a frame to help him plan how he wanted to offer this support. This frame is flexible and fits the needs of both teachers and students. However, the following planning questions in table 4.8 helped him focus the support.

Questions to Guide Implementing Strategic Learning Practice, Climate 3:

Each and every student is supported by a collaborative academic environment that enhances student productivity.

Use these planning questions to focus your support.

	Notes
❑ What skill will my students learn, and how will they demonstrate they have learned it?	
❑ How will I ensure an academic environment?	
❑ What opportunities will I plan for authentic collaboration?	
❑ What opportunities will I plan to allow for collaborative behaviors?	
❑ What opportunities will I plan to support individual student productivity specific to the learning outcome?	
❑ How will I share this information with my students?	
❑ How will I check that my students understand the impact of scholarly behaviors on their learning?	
❑ How will my students understand that reflecting on their scholarly behaviors supports ownership of their learning?	

Table 4.8: Questions to Guide Implementing Strategic Learning Practice, Climate 3

Implementing the Practice

How did Mr. Schoonover use the questions in table 4.8 to help plan how he would offer support to his students? First, he had to determine the following:

▸ What skill will my students learn, and how will they demonstrate they have learned it?

Mr. Schoonover says, "We are finishing up the unit on energy. We have already constructed explanations about energy, made observations about how energy can be transferred, and predicted outcomes about changes in energy. We are now ready for performance expectation 4-PS3-4: 'Apply scientific ideas to design, test, and refine a device that converts energy from one form to another.' Given a problem to solve, students will work in groups to collaboratively design a solution that converts energy from one form to another. They must work together to do this. Afterward, each student will then write an explanatory essay describing the process of solving the problem, how they designed a solution, and what results they got."

Mr. Schoonover also had to determine the following:

▸ How will I ensure an academic environment?

Mr. Schoonover continues, "Aside from having all of the materials and resources needed for the experiment, I need my students to have a scientific mindset. The science practices help me determine what this looks like. We are focusing on how scientists ask questions and define problems; construct explanations and design solutions; and obtain, evaluate, and communicate information. We have discussed, modeled, and practiced them. Now they are ready to apply. But most importantly, I need my students to understand that most scientists work with other scientists. Collaboration is key."

Mr. Schoonover next had to determine the answers to the following questions:

▸ What opportunities will I plan for authentic collaboration?

▸ What opportunities will I plan to allow for collaborative behaviors?

Mr. Schoonover explains, "I needed a project that demanded my students work together. I also wanted it to be loosely constructed so that they had to determine what they would do, how they would do it, and what materials they would need. I learned about a great project from a colleague at another school. The students first had to determine as a team what to construct. The options were to build a machine that does one of the following: move a Ping-Pong ball at least one yard, ring a bell, or increase the water level in a vase by one inch. The machine's design had to meet certain requirements. It had to show at least three different energy conversions, use at least two different forms of energy, and demonstrate the energy conversions and different forms of energy.

"This project was perfect for my class because they would have to collaborate every step of the way to make decisions—how to review what they already knew, how to determine the aim of their machine, how to build the machine, and how to test it. If it didn't work or they made a mistake, they would have to work together to start over."

Mr. Schoonover then had to ask himself the following question:

▶ What opportunities will I plan to support individual student productivity specific to the learning outcome?

Mr. Schoonover says, "The students would work together on the model and would receive a collective score based on rubrics—one rubric for the project and one for the collaborative effort. However, for the individual learning, I needed each of them to write an explanatory essay on the process of this experiment. During the collaborative group work, students needed to take their own notes on the project. The essay would also include a reflection section on their learning and on the group work."

Mr. Schoonover then had to determine the following:

▶ How will I share this information with my students?

▶ How will I check that my students understand the impact of scholarly behaviors on their learning?

Mr. Schoonover goes on, "At the beginning of each unit, we discuss the authentic application and final product of the unit. So my students already knew that they were going to be working as a team to solve a problem and build a machine but that they would write their own essays. I also showed them the collaborative behaviors rubric we would use to score the teamwork. We discussed each of the rubric's sections: Team Management, Problem-Solving Skills, Effort and Support, Positive Attitude."

Mr. Schoonover finally determined the following:

▸ How will my students understand that reflecting on their scholarly behaviors supports ownership of their learning?

Mr. Schoonover notes, "The students would use the collaborative behaviors rubric to self-assess, with evidence, their strengths and areas of growth. They would also score one another, with evidence, on the same criteria. The final section of their essay would include a reflection on the process, their learning, and the value of teamwork. Even though they are still in elementary school, it is not too early to get them thinking about college and a possible career in science. Owning these behaviors puts my students in the shoes of a scientist and lets them experience what this is like."

Teachers like Mr. Schoonover have realized that without this support— multiple opportunities to work together and grapple as a team, reflect on their efforts as a team member, and reflect on their ultimate learning by working on a team—his students would struggle with owning their learning.

What Teachers Are Doing

What are other ways teachers have implemented this practice—"Each and every student is supported by a **collaborative academic environment** that **enhances student productivity**"—as they offer support for developing student ownership?

Take this example from a high school English teacher: "Even though my students are older, they still need to be reminded how to work in a group. At the beginning of the year, we develop our team norms. Typically, we come up with some variation of the following norms: everybody helps, give reasons for your suggestions, no one is done until everyone is done, you have the right to ask anyone in your group for help, you have the duty to assist anyone who asks for help, and no one is as smart as all of us together. The kids make posters of the norms that hang up in the room all year. I monitor teamwork and point to the poster when I see a team not working well or to promote the positive behaviors."

Take this example from a sixth-grade history teacher: "My students struggle with group work unless it is super structured and each member has a role. I tend to use the roles of facilitator, resource manager, recorder, and time-keeper. The facilitator manages the work and is the one who talks with the teacher. The resource manager gathers and keeps track of all needed materials. The recorder writes down important information and group decisions. The timekeeper keeps track of the time for the group. All members are expected to take their own notes. At the beginning of the year, I assign the groups and the roles. With practice, the students take over more and more of the decision-making."

Take this example from a fifth-grade teacher: "I have started incorporating more and more collaboration into my classroom. There have been many amazing outcomes from this work, but one of the best is that my students now see one another as learning resources. This was a previously untapped resource in my class. Each student brings new ideas and ways of thinking that stretch everyone else's ideas and thinking. This didn't happen overnight. We did a lot of work cultivating this thinking and building an environment in which sharing our thinking was a must. My students have learned to depend on their peers."

What Students Are Saying

What do students say about this practice—"Each and every student is supported by a **collaborative academic environment** that **enhances student productivity**"—and its support for the ownership of their learning?

Take this example from an eleventh-grade student: "My teacher tells us we all have learning strengths. I like it when we do collaborative work because we get to work from our strengths. When we are given a task, we go through several steps. We first determine the problem, then we share what we think may be possible solutions. From there we have to outline a plan or approach. At this point, we also share what we think our strengths are specific to this task. Knowing my strengths and where I need support from others will definitely help me in college and when I get a job. That's what the real world is all about."

Take this example from an eighth grader: "In my science class, we do group tests sometimes. These tests are harder than the regular ones. We could never do well on our own, but together we can figure it out. I wouldn't want group tests every time because they are hard. But it can be fun to work together and solve the problems. We get to use one another and any resources we have in our classroom."

Climate Reflection

How Well Do You Develop Students to Own Their Role in the Class?

In this chapter, we have shown you what student ownership looks like in practice. We have shown you what it sounds like when students own their part in climate. And we have given examples of how teachers have implemented these strategic learning practices in a variety of classrooms.

We have also explained the difference between a student who is simply *doing* or *understanding* climate and one who is *owning* their role in the class.

A student is *doing* when they can state the rules of the classroom.

A student is *understanding* when they can explain how a respectful, cooperative, and collaborative class supports their learning.

A student is *owning* their role in the class when they can articulate their role in a respectful, cooperative, and collaborative environment; how scholarly behaviors support their own learning; and how they can develop this environment and these behaviors for future use.

Think of your students. Where do they fall on the doing-understanding-owning continuum? Think about the supports they need from you to develop student ownership. How often and to what degree do you offer these supports? In other words, what impact do you have on student ownership?

Remember that John Hattie (2011) said: "Such passion for evaluating impact is the single most critical lever for instructional excellence—accompanied by understanding this impact, and doing something in light of the evidence and understanding" (p. viii).

What follows are reflection activities that will help you determine your impact on student ownership—both in areas of strength and in areas of growth.

In order to develop student ownership, all student learning is driven by a positive academic climate. And, as always, your actions are key to the development of student ownership.

Reflect on Strategic Learning Practice, Climate 1

Each and every student is supported by a respectful academic environment that recognizes and promotes scholarly behaviors.

Consider how your students respond to the following questions:

- ▸ What is your role in the class?
- ▸ How do you recognize and promote others?
- ▸ What scholarly behaviors support your learning?

Think about your students' responses—remembering that your support is directly linked to developing student ownership—and use the following to help you reflect on the strengths and gaps of your support.

How often and how well do you offer these supports?

- Interactions are focused on recognizing and promoting students academically and build toward mastery of the relevant standards and measurable and achievable learning outcomes.

_____

- The teacher interacts with all students in an academic, respectful, and supportive manner.

_____

- Students interact with one another and the teacher in an academic, respectful, and supportive manner.

_____

- Positive academic interactions are made public.

Table 4.9: Reflect on Strategic Learning Practice, Climate 1

Reflect on Strategic Learning Practice, Climate 2

Each and every student is supported by a cooperative academic environment that encourages risk taking.

Consider how your students respond to the following questions:

▸ How do you support others in their learning?

▸ How do you take academic risks?

▸ What is the value of taking academic risks?

Think about your students' responses—remembering that your support is directly linked to developing student ownership—and use the following to help you reflect on the strengths and gaps of your support.

How often and how well do you offer these supports?

• Authentic cooperative activities build toward mastery of the relevant standards and measurable and achievable learning outcomes.

_____

• Interactions encourage students to take academic chances.

_____

• Interactions facilitate students to ask for help from the teacher and other students.

_____

• Interactions support a willingness to make academic mistakes.

Table 4.10: Reflect on Strategic Learning Practice, Climate 2

Reflect on Strategic Learning Practice, Climate 3

Each and every student is supported by a collaborative academic environment that enhances student productivity.

Consider how your students respond to the following questions:

▸ How do you work with other students?

▸ What is the value of working as a team?

▸ How does working on a team support your learning?

Think about your students' responses—remembering that your support is directly linked to developing student ownership—and use the following to help you reflect on the strengths and gaps of your support.

How often and how well do you offer these supports?

- Authentic collaborative activities build toward mastery of the relevant standards and measurable and achievable learning outcomes.

_____

- Interactions facilitate sharing and mutual respect among all students.

_____

- Interactions promote interdependence in students' academic productivity.

_____

- Interactions lead to increased individual academic productivity.

Table 4.11: Reflect on Strategic Learning Practice, Climate 3

CONCLUSION

Motivating Students to Own Their Learning

Imagine walking into a classroom where all students were motivated to know what they are learning, how they are learning, how well they are learning, and their role in the learning. Imagine if they were motivated to share this information with others. Imagine if this motivation led students to determine the steps needed to elevate academic achievement. We'd say we were in a classroom full of students who owned their learning. We'd say we'd want to teach that class.

We can.

Educators know that student motivation is a key to greater academic success. We believe that motivation can be taught. We have shown how any teacher is able to increase student motivation, and thus student achievement, by increasing student ownership.

Throughout this book we have:

- ▶ defined student ownership,
- ▶ explained what it could look like and sound like in a classroom,
- ▶ identified the teacher's role in developing student ownership, and
- ▶ determined the most critical supports needed to develop student ownership.

Using a variety of research about what best supports students to increase ownership of their learning, we developed a set of strategic learning practices that should be offered to students on a daily basis. While there are hundreds of actions a teacher must take in a day, this book focused on those practices in curriculum, instruction, assessment, and climate that actually increase the opportunities for learning—and increase the opportunities for student ownership.

The strategic learning practices in each area are as follows:

Curriculum

- **Strategic Learning Practice, Curriculum 1:** Each and every student is supported by relevant standards with measurable and achievable outcomes that are accessible and that drive all learning.

- **Strategic Learning Practice, Curriculum 2:** Each and every student is supported by units and lessons that provide an integrated approach and that support conceptual redundancy of the learning outcomes.

- **Strategic Learning Practice, Curriculum 3:** Each and every student is supported by access to curriculum materials that match the content and rigor of the learning outcomes.

Instruction

- **Strategic Learning Practice, Instruction 1:** Each and every student is supported by opportunities for meaningful engagement using structured student-to-student communication.

- **Strategic Learning Practice, Instruction 2:** Each and every student is supported by opportunities for meaningful engagement using effective instructional strategies.

- **Strategic Learning Practice, Instruction 3:** Each and every student is supported by opportunities for meaningful engagement in which instructional time is used efficiently.

Assessment

- **Strategic Learning Practice, Assessment 1:** Each and every student is supported by data that is used to monitor current understanding and provide feedback.

- **Strategic Learning Practice, Assessment 2:** Each and every student is supported by data that is used to monitor current understanding and adjust as needed.

- **Strategic Learning Practice, Assessment 3:** Each and every student is supported by data that is used to differentiate based on predetermined student needs.

Climate

- **Strategic Learning Practice, Climate 1:** Each and every student is supported by a respectful academic environment that recognizes and promotes scholarly behaviors.

- **Strategic Learning Practice, Climate 2:** Each and every student is supported by a cooperative academic environment that encourages risk taking.

- **Strategic Learning Practice, Climate 3:** Each and every student is supported by a collaborative academic environment that enhances student productivity.

Integrating the Practices

Not one of these practices in curriculum, instruction, assessment, and climate can be implemented in isolation. In fact, their power is in the integration of one with the other, because each practice directly impacts the others. It is the teacher's job to decide how these practices work together to ensure the highest likelihood of student learning. As we have stated over and over, the teacher's strength is in their decision-making. Designing and delivering and reflecting on a course, a unit, and a lesson that is effective and efficient and that supports increased student ownership is paramount.

Let's revisit that third-grade classroom we visited in the introduction of this book and view it from the point of view of the teacher's decisions and actions.

Remember what that third grader answered when we asked, "What are you learning?"

"Today I am learning how to describe characters by their traits, motivations, and feelings. We are reading *Charlotte's Web*, and I am describing Wilbur in chapter 3. I will know that I have done a good job taking notes on this by filling out my character map accurately. I am learning how to do this because, when we finish the book, I am writing an opinion essay on which character was most admirable: Charlotte, Wilbur, or Fern. I will take notes on all of the characters to use as details in my essay. I am checking with my friends in my group because they will help me figure out if I have left any important information out of my notes. I will help them because that's how we help everybody in the class get smarter. I like working in groups because the talking helps me better understand what I am thinking. I like this classroom because I get smarter every day."

This is a clear example of a student who owns their learning. This student can articulate what they are learning, why they are learning it, how they will demonstrate they have learned it, how they are learning it, and how they will work together with other students to support one another.

For this student to be able to explain as they did, it is clear they were supported by the implementation of the strategic learning practices. Notice the plural. The power of these practices is their ability to integrate and build on one another. This third-grade student was supported by **relevant standards** with a **measurable and achievable outcome** that was **accessible** and that **drove all learning** (Curriculum 1) within a lesson and unit that provided an **integrated approach** (Curriculum 2) using **materials that matched the content and rigor of the learning outcome** (Curriculum 3). The student had many **opportunities for meaningful engagement** using **structured student-to-student communication** (Instruction 1) and **effective instructional strategies** (Instruction 2) while **receiving and providing feedback** (Assessment 1). This student was also supported by an **academic classroom climate** that is **respectful** (Climate 1), that is **cooperative**, and that **encouraged risk taking** (Climate 2) by having students share their strengths and challenges with one another.

The teacher's integration of these practices was the most supportive decision she could have made for her students.

Let's look at a high school biology class and see how this teacher integrated the practices.

"When my students walk in the classroom, the objective is always listed on the board. The objective includes the skill being learned (*what*) and the success criteria (*how* and *demonstrate*). I go over the objective and then have my students discuss it with A-B partners. Partner A shares what they are going to learn, and Partner B shares how they will demonstrate the learning. I call on random students to make sure we are all clear about today's learning. This takes about two minutes. But I need them to take a stronger role in understanding the learning for today—I need them to take ownership. I then ask two questions. The first is: 'How many of you can demonstrate the learning right now?' One or two hands might go up. The second is: 'How many of you feel confident that you will be able to demonstrate the learning by the end of the lesson?' Normally all hands go up. This gets them into the mindset that they have a role in the learning, and I find they are more willing to take risks."

In the first five minutes of class, this teacher decided to support these students by offering a **measurable and achievable outcome** that was **accessible** and that **drove all learning** (Curriculum 1). The students then had **opportunities for meaningful engagement** using **structured student-to-student communication** (Instruction 1) and while **receiving and providing feedback** (Assessment 1). Students were also supported by an **academic classroom climate** that was **respectful** (Climate 1), that was **cooperative**, and that **encouraged risk taking** (Climate 2) by having them share their readiness to learn.

These are just two examples of going beyond merely *doing* or *understanding* school—these are examples of students *owning* their learning. A student who owns their learning can state what they are learning and why, can explain how they learn best, can articulate when they are learning and when they are struggling, and understands their role in any academic setting.

Building the Mindset of Student Ownership

We have defined student ownership as a mindset: a mindset of those students who know they have the authority, the capacity, and the responsibility to own their learning.

We have shown that the most efficient and effective manner to build this mindset is for the teacher to model the thinking behind the ownership, explicitly teach the skills of ownership, and, most importantly, be willing to delegate the authority, capacity, and responsibility to the students.

Questions for Students

Students who possess an ownership mindset will be able to answer the following questions at any time during the course, unit, or lesson.

Regarding Curriculum:

- What am I learning?

- Why am I learning this?

- How will I demonstrate I have learned it?

Regarding Instruction:

- How will I learn this?

- How will this strategy help me learn this?

- How can I use this strategy in the future and in different situations?

Regarding Assessment:

- How will I know I have learned it?

- How will I know I am progressing in my learning?

- What can I do if I am struggling?

Regarding Climate:

- What is my role in the class?

- How will I support others in their learning?

- How will I take risks in my learning?

Table 5.1: Questions for Students

Questions for Teachers

Teachers who understand that their role is to build an ownership mindset with their students are able to explain how they decided the following information.

Regarding Curriculum:

- What will my students learn?

- Why are my students learning this?

- How will my students demonstrate they have learned it?

- How will I share these decisions with my students?

Regarding Instruction:

- How will my students learn this?

- How will this strategy help my students learn this?

- How will my students use this strategy in the future and in different situations?

- How will I share these decisions with my students?

Regarding Assessment:

- How will my students know they have learned this?

- How will my students know that they are progressing in their learning?

- What can my students do if they are struggling?

- How will I share these decisions with my students?

Regarding Climate:

- What is the student's role in the class?

- How will my students support others in their learning?

- How will my students take risks in their learning?

- How will I share these decisions with my students?

Table 5.2: Questions for Teachers

What Teachers Are Saying

Educators have let us know the impact these practices have made on their teaching and their students' learning.

The high school biology teacher explains: "As I began to implement the practice of ensuring all my students had a clear understanding of the learning outcome, I noted two significant changes. The first is that the students were more focused and attentive. I attribute this to the fact that they all understood the purpose of the lesson and the expectation of the learning. The second is that the classroom environment changed from 'I' and 'you' to a 'we.' We were in this together. With the learning outcome being so clear, the class began to work more as a unit toward the success criteria."

A middle school history teacher reflected: "When I began to work with the strategic learning practices, I began to reflect on the student engagement role in learning. I quickly realized I was doing all the work. I would read the content on the topic we were getting ready to learn. I would synthesize the information to determine the most pertinent content. I would cull the information down its most salient points. I would then share the content with the students, and they would take notes. I realized I was doing all the work and, possibly, all of the learning. I took a closer look at the verbs in the standards to find out what my students needed to do in order to demonstrate learning. I could not find 'copy the teacher's learning from the PowerPoint presentation' as a standard. I saw that they needed to learn to analyze and evaluate information. I decided I needed to release more of the learning to my students."

An elementary teacher summed it up: "My work with the strategic learning practices has completely changed my thinking. I used to think about what I was going to teach tomorrow. Now, I think about what my students need to learn tomorrow. My job is no longer about getting through the lesson. It is about getting through to the learners."

It is clear that each of these teachers works hard. We all work hard. We all come to school each day motivated to provide students with the highest-quality learning we can. But achievement can't be increased if only the teachers are motivated. Teachers need to ensure that the students are motivated to be active participants in their own learning. Taking ownership motivates students to increase their academic achievement in all areas. In this book, we have shown that this is something we can control.

Can you imagine walking into your own class full of motivated, engaged, and eager students who own their learning?

We can.

BIBLIOGRAPHY

Chan, P., Graham-Day, K. J., Ressa, V. A., Peters, M. T., & Konrad, M. (2014). Beyond involvement: Promoting student ownership of learning in classrooms. *Intervention in School and Clinic, 50*(2), 105–113.

Cornelius-White, J. (2007). Learner-centered teacher-student relationships are effective: A meta-analysis. *Review of Educational Research, 77*(1), 113–143.

Datta, D. K., & Narayanan, V. K. (1989). A meta-analytic review of the concentration-performance relationship: Aggregating findings in strategic management. *Journal of Management, 15*(3), 469–483.

Dunn, R., Griggs, S. A., Olson, J., Beasley, M., & Gorman, B. S. (1995). A meta-analytic validation of the Dunn and Dunn model of learning-style preferences. *Journal of Educational Research, 88*(6), 353–362.

Dusek, J. B., & Joseph, G. (1985). The bases of teacher expectancies. In J. B. Dusek (Ed.), *Teacher expectancies* (pp. 229–249). Hillsdale, NJ: Lawrence Erlbaum Associates.

Duzinski, G. A. (1987). *The educational utility of cognitive behavior modification strategies with children: A quantitative synthesis* (Unpublished doctoral dissertation). University of Illinois, Chicago, IL.

Fendick, F. (1990). *The correlation between teacher clarity of communication and student achievement gain: A meta-analysis* (Unpublished doctoral dissertation). University of Florida, FL.

Fuchs, L. S. & Fuchs, D. (1986). Curriculum-based assessment of progress toward long-term and short-term goals. *Journal of Special Education, 20*(1), 69–82.

Fuchs, L. S., & Fuchs, D. (1986). Effects of systematic formative evaluation: A meta-analysis. *Exceptional Children, 53*(3), 199–208.

Haertel, G. D., Walberg, H. J., & Haertel, E. H. (1981). Socio-psychological environments and learning: A quantitative synthesis. *British Educational Research Journal, 7*(1), 27–36.

Hattie, J. (2009). *Visible learning: A synthesis of over 800 meta-analyses relating to achievement*. Oxford, UK: Routledge.

Hattie, J. (2011). *Visible Learning for Teachers*. Oxford, UK: Routledge.

Hattie, J., & Timperley, H. (2007). The power of feedback. *Review of Educational Research, 77*(1), 81–112.

Huang, Z. (1991). *A meta-analysis of self-questioning strategies* (Unpublished doctoral dissertation). Hofstra University, Long Island, NY.

Hunter, M. (1967). *Teach more—faster!* Thousand Oaks, CA: Corwin.

Hunter, M. (1982). *Mastery teaching*. El Segundo, CA: TIP Publications.

Kluger, A. N., & DeNisi, A. (1996). The effects of feedback interventions on performance: A historical review, a meta-analysis, and a preliminary feedback intervention theory. *Psychological Bulletin, 119*(2), 254–284.

Kulhavy, R. W. (1977). Feedback in written instruction. *Review of Educational Research, 47*(2), 211–232.

Kumar, D. D. (1991). A meta-analysis of the relationship between science instruction and student engagement. *Educational Review, 43*(1), 49–61.

Locke, E. A., & Latham, G. P. (1990). *A theory of goal setting and task performance*. Englewood Cliffs, NJ: Prentice Hall.

Marzano, R. J. (1998). *A theory-based meta-analysis of research on instruction*. Aurora, CO: Mid-Continent Regional Educational Lab.

Marzano, R. J. (2000). *A new era of school reform: Going where the research takes us*. Aurora, CO: Mid-Continent Regional Educational Lab.

National Center on Scaling Up Effective Schools. (2014). *Developing student ownership and responsibility in high schools* (Practitioner brief). Nashville, TN: National Center on Scaling Up Effective Schools.

Newell, A. (1990). *Unified theories of cognition*. Cambridge, MA: Harvard University Press.

Nuthall, G. (2005). The cultural myths and realities of classroom teaching and learning: A personal journey. *Teachers College Record, 107*(5), 895–934.

Nuthall, G. (2007). *The hidden lives of learners*. Wellington, New Zealand: NZCER Press.

O'Connell, M. J., & Vandas, K. (2015). *Partnering with students: Building ownership of learning*. Thousand Oaks, CA: Corwin.

Purkey, W. W. (1992). An introduction to invitational theory. *Journal of Invitational Theory and Practice, 1*(1), 5–15.

Robinson, V. (2011). *Student-centered leadership*. San Francisco, CA: Jossey-Bass.

Rosenshine, B., & Meister, C. (1994). Reciprocal teaching: A review of the research. *Review of Educational Research, 64*(4), 479–530.

Samson, G. E., Strykowski, B., Weinstein, T., & Walberg, H. J. (1987). The effects of teacher questioning levels on student achievement: A quantitative synthesis. *Journal of Educational Research, 80*(5), 290–295.

Seidel T., & Shavelson, R. J. (2007). Teaching effectiveness research in the past decade: The role of theory and research design in disentangling meta-analysis results. *Review of Educational Research, 77*(4), 454–499.

Stevens, R. J., & Slavin, R. E. (1990). When cooperative learning improves the achievement of students with mild disabilities: A response to Tateyama-Sniezek. *Exceptional Children, 57*(3), 276–280.

Swanson, H. L., & Hoskyn, M. (1998). Experimental intervention research on students with learning disabilities: A meta-analysis of treatment outcomes. *Review of Educational Research, 68*(3), 277–321.

Timperley, H. (2011). *Realizing the power of professional learning*. New York, NY: Open University Press.

Walker, D., Greenwood, C., Hart, B., & Carta, J. (1994). Prediction of school outcomes based on early language production and socioeconomic factors. *Child Development, 65*(2), 606–621.

Wiggins, G., & McTighe, J. (2005). *Understanding by design* (2nd ed.). Alexandria, VA: Association for Supervision and Curriculum Development.